Create the Life Your Want

And How a Coach Can Help

11 Expert Life Coaches Share How to Create the Life, Career, or Business You Want

Co-authored by members of the International Association of Professional Life Coaches®

Compiled By Jeannette Koczela

ISBN: 978-1-7926-5632-3

Table of Contents

Forward

In the following chapters of this book, you will hear from our co-authors about how life coaching can enhance your life and help you create the life you want.

Each chapter has insights, techniques, and informative narratives on how coaching can help you change your life.

A life coach is not a mentor, therapist or counselor but rather a professional who works with clients, helping them to set personal and/or professional goals, overcome obstacles or make necessary changes in their lives. They do so by *partnering* with their clients to set desired goals, experience personal growth, or make behavior modifications.

As you read through these chapters, we hope this book gives you the information and motivation to hire a coach for yourself.

As coaches, we want to partner with you in a way that transforms your passion for your dreams into action for your life.

You can find a listing of coaches to choose from in our Life Coach Directory at www.iaplifecoaches.org/life-coach-directory

"How to Survive and Thrive at Today's Version of the Game of Life ™"

By Sandra Hill

Remember the popular board game, The Game of Life™, originally created by Milton Bradley? This game simulates the life events many people go through... from going to college, getting married, raising a family, buying a home, working and eventually retiring. The players moved in a fairly linear path, with a few intersections where they can go one way or another and make choices regarding investments and insurance. However, it is essentially a game of luck.

As a pre-teen, I played this game more than a dozen times and always loved it. It seemed so easy and was always great fun to move past milestones and gain money and other assets. As I got older though, I soon realized that The Game of Life™ (Game) and the reality of life (Reality) were totally different from each other. Reality has many twists and turns and some deep, deep crevasses that a person can fall into. While people journeyed through the Game in a linear manner, it was not the same with Reality. Instead people crisscrossed, went in circles, traversed in all different directions and sometimes even spiraled out of control. In fact, I found that REALITY HAD NO INSTRUCTIONS *or, so it seemed.*

When Reality gets overwhelming

Have you ever left on a business trip and upon landing or getting to the event, learn about an emergency at your office or at home that needed to be dealt with? You had to shift gears, handle it, regroup and – hopefully - get to your destination (frazzled and late, of course).

Have you ever gone to the store to run an errand and arrived home only to find that you STILL hadn't gotten the item that you originally intended to pick up? Do you end up getting annoyed with yourself?

Do you 'think' you put your wallet in the gym locker or your car's glove compartment but can't seem to locate it? After dealing with the initial panic, you call and cancel all your cards and suddenly it hits you, you have a new gym bag and had slid your wallet in a side pocket. Do you feel embarrassed? Upset? Irritated by your forgetfulness?

Or, maybe you are on your way home after an exhausting day and your car breaks down during rush hour traffic on the expressway! You call for a tow service, assuming something is wrong with your vehicle, only to be told when they arrive that you were actually just out of gas. Too busy or sidetracked to notice the gas needle??

Summer vacation has rolled around and you and your family are packing up for a road trip. Suddenly, you realize you forgot to make reservations. You frantically start calling around only to find that everything is booked solid. Hopefully this hasn't happened to you, because it happened to me and it was not fun!

You see, I had been overly busy. I was overwhelmed with life. I was frustrated. Sometimes life happens, and we don't like how we feel or how we react. I know you've had your moments.

Have you ever done some type of internal assessment and tried to figure out how to get your life back in order on your own? Have you ever wanted to shout at the top of your lungs, "GET ME BACK ON TRACK, SOMEONE... ANYONE... PLEASE!!"

We have all been 'there' but we don't have to be 'there' alone. We don't have to wait until we hit a wall to try to climb up and over that temporary hurdle. These events are wake up calls and sometimes, that is just what we need to realize that we need help, some instruction or guidance. Unbeknownst to most of us though, we have access to instructions. They come to us in the form of **life coaching.**

"Life isn't about finding yourself. Life is about creating yourself."
- George Bernard Shaw

But, exactly what *IS* life coaching?

Life coaching is a process in which a coach helps those who are at crossroads gain back what they feel is missing from their life, career or business. A life coach offers support and guidance to those who are feeling stuck, confused or overwhelmed. A life coach helps those who know there is something more that they want in their lives and who are ready to take action and move past the barriers that have been holding them back.

A life coach is not a mentor, therapist or counselor but a professional who works with clients, helping them to move forward and set personal and/or professional goals, overcome obstacles, or make changes in their lives. They do so by *partnering* with their clients to set desired goals, experience personal growth, or make behavior modifications.

The benefits of life coaching are tremendous. Working with a life coach can help you:
   ❖ See and feel tangible results, almost immediately
   ❖ Be held accountable
   ❖ Feel more fulfilled
   ❖ Become more engaging and enjoy life again

❖ Get a step-by-step process for how to reach your desired goal(s)

So, who is life coaching for?

Life coaching is for business professionals, aspiring managers and leaders, working parents returning to the job market after an extended absence, students and recent graduates, entrepreneurs, veterans transitioning to a civilian lifestyle, moms- and dads-to-be, artists, adults with ADHD, and retirees. In fact, life coaching can be for anyone.

On the ROAD called LIFE

You have to take the GOOD with the BAD,
Smile with the SAD.
 Love what you got,
  And remember what you had.
ALWAYS forgive but NEVER forget.
LEARN from your mistakes, but NEVER forget.

PEOPLE change; THINGS go wrong,
But just remember…THE RIDE GOES ON!

Figure 1: Roadmap courtesy of PIXABY

Rough Patches

Reduce Stress and Anxiety

I would like to introduce you to Alice. Alice *was* a stay-at-home Mom who recently lost her husband. Now needing to support herself and her three children, Alice needed to get a job. However, it couldn't be just any job. In order to support her young family, she had to get a <u>good</u> paying job with benefits like healthcare, vision, dental and a retirement plan. You see, Alice's husband didn't work long enough at any one company to have anything other than basic dental, health and vision insurance.

Naturally, Alice was fretful and quite anxious. She had gone to college and majored in Art History. Her only paying jobs up to this point were babysitting, dog walking and housesitting years ago while she was in college. Because of the nature of those jobs, Alice had never even had to prepare a resume or even been on a formal job interview. She was also overwhelmed because her children had begun to act out. Luckily, the school they attended had a great counseling program, which was free.

As Alice waited to meet with the counselors and get her children signed up for the program, she came across an article while flipping through a magazine in the waiting area. She felt goosebumps as she read a few of the highlights – *Feeling under pressure? ...not knowing where to turn" Don't feel you have what it takes?* ... Alice took a picture of the pages and made a mental note to contact the agency that claimed to specialize in life coaching. They guaranteed success, and that was what she needed, sooner rather than later.

Fast forward by a few weeks and Alice is no longer feeling anxious and fretful about her situation. In fact, she has a positive demeanor and feels like she has a sense of purpose. Her walk and speech are different. She has an air of confidence that she hadn't felt in years. She had only seen her life coach three or four times, but in that short time she had not only learned some coping techniques but, with the support from the coach, found the courage to go back to school and take courses that qualified her for a position that was opening at a local bank.

Here's a few things Alice learned from her coaching sessions:
- ❖ **Journaling** – By writing her thoughts down, Alice became more aware of her own feelings, frustrations, wants and desires. Working with a life coach who asked deep, probing questions, Alice gained insights about herself. At times she came to conclusions that scared her and took her out of her comfort zone, but as her coach reminded her: do not feed your fears!

❖ **Meditation** - By meditating daily, Alice realized that she was doing better than she thought in life. Why? Through completing a series of exercises, she found that she had a growing list of things to be thankful for, like having a roof over her head, food to eat, clean water to drink and healthy children. Alice's gratitude list kept growing and she now understood that, no matter what, there were those who were less fortunate than she was and that she should focus on what she did have instead of what she was lacking.

❖ **Setting goals** – Before learning how to set SMART (specific, measurable, attainable, realistic, timely) goals, Alice was quite overwhelmed with all that she needed to get done in order just to keep herself afloat. She learned about priorities, the types of goals and goal setting.

❖ **Investing in her own self-development** – Alice learned that she had to take care of herself before working on anyone else. She learned to absorb what was useful and to discard what was not. Most importantly, she learned how to dream. As Napoleon Hill once said, "WHATEVER THE MIND OF MAN CAN CONCEIVE AND BELIEVE, IT CAN ACHIEVE."

❖ **Trusting herself** – Alice learned to 'listen to her heart' and trust her own instinct. She realized that listening to and trusting her own inner wisdom, especially when she felt frazzled, helped her become more centered and clearer on what she needed to do.

❖ **Becoming open to possibilities** – This was probably one of the most important and difficult life coaching concepts Alice had to develop. Her life coach told her during their free consultation that there would be moments of uncertainty where Alice was going to have to be willing to step outside her comfort zone. Alice was terrified of the unknown, just like you and me. However, Alice's desire to change, feel better about herself and make better decisions was the driving force that helped her move forward to her desired end state.

❖ **How to handle fearful moments**– Alice learned how not to "feed her fears" because they caused her to make excuses. Most importantly, Alice learned how to let go of things she couldn't control!

Each and every day, Alice repeated this quote from *Nelson Mandela: "It always seems impossible until it's done."*

Life coaching can help you get over the rough patches on the life's bumpy highway. Do you have some rough patches that need mending?

Finding Yourself

Sometimes life gives you everything a person could want – or so it seems. In Bradley's case, he didn't want to be known as the guy "who was born with a silver spoon in his mouth." He didn't want to follow in his father's footsteps and take over the family business. The problem was, Bradley didn't know *what* he wanted, he just knew what he *didn't* want.

His father thought he was a lost cause, but a family friend suggested that he seek out a life coach for his son. She had hired one for herself and the coach helped her tremendously. The father, who was intrigued and a bit surprised that his friend had a life coach, decided to give it a try. To his surprise, he learned that he really didn't even know his own son. As his son began working with the coach, he became a completely different person and transformed right before his father's eyes.

You see, through the coaching process, Bradley learned more about himself than even *he* ever knew. He completed a personality and emotional intelligence assessment and worked through various exercises that caused him to visualize and do some serious introspection. Most importantly, Bradley learned how to assert himself. After practicing various role-playing scenarios, Bradley was able to better articulate, to his father, what he wanted out of life. Bradley even asked his father to participate in some joint coaching sessions so that his dad would better understand him.

Over time, the dad accepted his son's decision to invest in some non-profits and not have an active role in the family business. Bradley finally felt fulfilled; his life had a purpose. And, as they began to bond, the son periodically invited his father to give advice and suggestions. At the same time, his dad learned how to create space for his son, which, in turn, caused Bradley to feel more empowered to live his own life and make his own decisions.

Bradley learned to give himself permission to try something new because he knew he was becoming the best person he could possibly be.

Gaining Self-Confidence

Twins Twanda and L'Swanda were identical and did EVERYTHING together, that is, until they both graduated from college with business degrees and got recruited for high-powered jobs in different cities. Their parents were overjoyed, but the twins were not. They both had a fear of the unknown and couldn't bear the thought of being apart. Even with the ability to easily communicate regularly thanks to technology, the young women had never lived apart and felt that their world would crumble without having the other one nearby. It became evident they needed some help coping with the changes.

Recognizing their fears, the women decided to pay a visit to the recruitment center at their old college campus and ask for support. What they got was much, much more than that. Each was assigned a life coach who met with them daily to help work through the relocation process. In separate sessions, each woman came to acknowledge her vulnerabilities while also acknowledging her uniqueness.

Over several weeks, they embarked on excursions down the road of life, working through scenarios, participating in exercises designed to help boost their confidence and self-esteem. The twins (sometimes independently, sometimes collectively) completed visualization exercises, started practicing skills designed to calm their inner critic, and completed a 100-day challenge.

By the end of their 30-day relocation period, both twins were in a better place mentally and physically. Continuing with their coaches, sessions became less frequent to allow the twins time to adjust to their new careers, while simultaneously putting into practice the various techniques they had learned from their respective coaches. Since they were in the same line of work, they kept in touch often to bounce ideas off each other and continue to support one another from afar using Facetime and the WhatsApp.

What the twins learned were the *Five W's of Life:*

> **WHO** you are makes you special so learn to appreciate that
> **WHAT** lies ahead is always a mystery, don't fear it
> **WHEN** life pushes you around, push back harder

WHERE there's a choice, make the one you won't regret
WHY doesn't always matter, shake it off and keep moving forward

It's All About Perspective

As far as his family was concerned, Charles III had everything going for him. If you asked Charles though, he wanted and needed more. Yes, he had a great career, a nice place to live, had enough income to pay the bills, but he had bigger dreams and knew there was something more for him.

He felt pigeon-holed at his current company, having been passed-over for promotion time and time again. He was a middle-aged man and felt he had lots to give to the company, if they would only give him the chance. He dreamed of running one of the European Markets and wanted to get a Ferrari now that his kids were all grown. He didn't understand why, after all of his years of service to this business, he was not being considered for more senior roles as they became available.

So, Charles sought out the services of a life coach to help him get that dream job. To his dismay though, after the first consult, the coach wanted him to take some assessments designed to identify his personality type, communication style and type of leadership style he preferred as well as displayed. Charles didn't think any of these assessments were necessary, so he refused.

Charles wanted the coach to fix the situation. Charles knew he had agreed to be open to coaching, after all, he had signed an agreement identifying the coaching expectations. However, when the time came to put in the work, Charles told the coach it was a waste of his time.

It wasn't until Charles had an epiphany... an Ah-ha moment... that things started to click. Since the meetings were in-person, the coach simply started mirroring everything Charles said and did. Charles kept wondering why the coach was acting in such a non-professional manner, so one day he asked the coach. The coach asked Charles to list all of the negative behaviors and tendencies he saw the coach doing and saying.

Charles then had to read the list out loud. Mid-way through the list, Charles face changed, and he muttered something unintelligible. When the coach asked Charles to speak up, he said, "You were mocking me! This is not you. It's... me. Do I REALLY act that way and say those things? Wow! I wasn't aware that was the way I come across to people."

From that moment forward, Charles became more aware of aspects that he didn't like about himself and was now completely set on making changes. And with the help of his coach, he became the change he wanted to see. Over time, through self-development work with his coach, he learned how to interact with people, communicate professionally and be more accepting and empathetic.

He also started mentoring the newer, less-experienced employees. He became more respectful towards his younger bosses, so much so that one of them recommended Charles to help out when an employee's unexpected illness left the company in a vulnerable position.

Not only did Charles step up to the plate, he put his best foot forward and didn't "act out" after the person he temporarily replaced eventually came back to work. Charles was in a better place and knew it. So, when he was called into his boss' office and told he was going to receive a "well-deserved" pay raise, Charles became overjoyed and quite emotional.

Things might not have gone as well for Charles had he refused to be an active participant in his transformation. With coaching, the process starts with YOU. If you are not willing and don't commit to the process, then it will be a waste of your time.

How much do you want to advance in life? Do you want to gain a better lifestyle, become more valued and respected? Do you want to feel better about yourself and improve your communication with others? Allow yourself to HOPE, to BELIEVE and to TRUST again. Don't let a few bad memories stop you from having a good life NOW. We are all works in progress. Life Coaching can help you, you just have to give it a try.

How To Find The Right Life Coach

Finding a life coach to work with can be relatively easy. You can search for them on Google or visit an online coach directory, such as the IAPLC, to browse coaches by category. Most coaches will offer a free consultation, so the both of you can figure out if you a good fit for each other. Just like when you are shopping for a new car, you can give the coach a test drive, which is an important step in finding the right person to work with.

It's best to consult with a few different coaches, to get an idea of what kind of coaching style and process will best suit your needs. When it comes to choosing a coach, having a good connection with them is one of the most important things – you want to ensure you feel comfortable with this person and can be open with them. Coaching can be a very emotional process, so feeling safe and connected to your coach will allow you to get more out of the sessions.

Before seeking out a life coach, you need to figure out what you are looking for in a coach. Here are some questions you should ask yourself:

- ❖ Do you want a male or female coach? Do you have an age preference?
- ❖ Do you want to meet face-to-face or is working over the phone or virtually okay?
- ❖ How much support do you want/need?
- ❖ What other traits would you want the coach to have?

Once you set up a consultation with the coach(es), you should ask them:

- ❖ About their methodology – Do they give homework or perform career and personality assessments? How often do they want to meet? What kind of process do they use?
- ❖ What is their communication style? Does it jell with yours?
- ❖ How accessible are they? Do they offer check-ins between sessions?
- ❖ Does the coach "get" you and seem to understand your problem/situation/circumstance?

Another great way to find a coach is through word of mouth or referrals from such individuals like your employer, friend or relative. If you are looking to hire a coach for yourself, ask around and you'll likely find that people you know have hired their own at some point.

The great thing about life coaching is, it doesn't have to be done in person, meaning you can work with someone from another city, state or even another country!

Another way that you can find a life coach is by contacting me, yours truly. Just look at my biographical sketch, which follows.

Disclaimer: Some of the previous content appears in an upcoming book, publishing date to be announced.

About the Author

Sandra Hill

Raising children to a healthy, balanced adulthood can be challenging. Raising your own *and* helping to raise several other children can be even more daunting especially when they are pre-teens or teenagers. Before I even knew what coaching was, I found myself using certain aspects and techniques. As years progressed, my children and others were referring me to assist others.

So, when my organization wanted to become more engaged with coaching, I volunteered to be part of a pilot program. Not only did I successfully introduce a coaching culture, but I also created coaching programs for aspiring managers and those managers/leaders seeking advancement. I found that I had inadvertently discovered my passion and knew that after my 36 years of civil service I would one day become an entrepreneur and launch a coaching business.

I spent close to twenty years studying business and coaching books, learning from the school of professional experience before seeking out formal training and certification. And, after perfecting my coaching, relationship management and strategic planning skills I founded *New Horizen Coaching &*

Professional Growth Advancement. I also networked with several professional organizations where I became known for my success in helping business professional advance their careers. And, thus far tout a 98% success rate among my clients.

I am committed to providing the highest form of insight and guidance not only to those individuals and organizations who seek to advance their career, but also to those who seek to build their confidence, facilitate transitions in their personal or professional life, live a purposeful life or simple achieve work life balance. I use a proven framework that enables me to help prepare tomorrow's workforce.

Some of my workshops/training/motivational speaking topics are:

Be More Strategic
Be More Analytical
Become Empowered
Become More Articulate
Bolster Your Self Esteem
Coping Skills
Create Your Own Space
Elevator Pitch Writing
Getting a Handle on Procrastination
How to Control your Anger
Interview Preparation
Interview Skills Workshop
Time Management
Reduce Frustration
Resume Writing Workshops
Resume Reviews

My guiding principles also help me to maintain my focus and passion for 'making the impossible, possible' (the company's mantra). I conduct training and serve as a motivational speaker, have written several e-books and volunteer as a mentor to others. I am a fun-loving high-energy person who loves travelling and entertaining friends when not volunteering, working out, singing in my church's choir, gardening, cooking, making home-made crafts or sewing.

Want to stay in touch with what is new on the horizen? Here is how to reach me so you won't be left out of the cold when my online workshops and teleseminars launch or my newsletters is issued.

Website:	**www.newhorizencoaching.com**
Email:	**coachhill@newhorizencoaching.com**
Phone:	678-523-2890

As a bonus, I am offering a complimentary coaching session to you and two of your friends. Take the first step to increase your financial earnings by advancing your career. You'll feel less stressed and anxious, be more self-confident, learn how to communicate in a professional manner to get what you want and improve your relationships. There are much more benefits, but these are just a few of them. So, make an appointment today!

https://newhorizencoaching.com/contact/

"The Vital Ingredient For Weight Loss Success"

By Beverly Glazer

One of the most common mistakes people make, is that they think life coaching is another form of counseling ~ or that it is the same as getting therapy, but with an unlicensed professional. I am happy to tell you that this is a far cry from the truth. Life coaching is a unique service and although clients may achieve the same results, the method and the timeframe is different. Counseling is more in depth and lasts for an undetermined amount of time. But, in the coaching process, both client and coach work together to identify what the client needs, and there is an action plan to achieve it in a specified amount of time.

After earning a Masters Degree in Counselling Psychology, I specialized in all addictive behaviors. But, it was while I was studying eating disorders, that I discovered that I was a food addict too. Everyone has their little addictions, and food was 'my drug of choice'. According to *WCNC May 2017,* ninety-four per cent of teenage girls have been body shamed, and I was one of them.

My journey into the world of the diet industry began at an early age. I would read everything I could about weight and nutrition, followed the latest weight loss gurus and tried diligently to adhere to their restrictive diets, so I could look like the models in their ads. But I always failed. As soon as I veered off course, I lost control and the weight would come right back ~ and more. I felt guilty for having 'no willpower' and ashamed of myself for gaining back the weight. This led me to get back on the diet, and the roller-coaster of yo-yo dieting would start up once again. If you are an emotional eater, this is a familiar saga.

Back then, I believed that I'd be destined to count calories, fats and carbs or I'd suffer the consequences of lifetime of dieting. But that was not the case. Knowledge is power. So, the techniques I learned to help others, helped me to cure myself.

Today, I never count calories, nor am I threatened by a scale. I eat what I want, and whenever I want, and making healthy choices are effortless. All diet plans and specialists teach you what to do, but an emotional eater has already learned that. What they don't tell you is how to avoid doing what you do, so you don't sabotage yourself with food.

The U.S. **weight loss market** is estimated to be worth $68.2 billion in **2017**—a 2.7% **gain**, and **growth** should continue into 2018, when the **market** is expected to post a better **gain** of 3.2% to $70 billion. (MarketResearch Jan 2, 2018)

There is a vast amount of information and diet trends to follow, and if you are an emotional eater, your perception of weight loss and food has been distorted. To lose weight and sustain it, you must untwist all that diet propaganda from your mind. Once you shift your thinking, your behavior will also change, and you will successfully choose the foods that work for you.

Over the past 27 years I've counselled 1000s of clients, with all types of food issues, to stop binge eating, change bad habits, eat normally and ultimately lose weight. But private counselling is a long and expensive process. So, when I trained to add coaching to my practice, I was happy to discover that I could adapt the same successful techniques I've been using for years, into weight loss, personal and professional empowerment coaching programs, that take much less time. These step-by-step systems are not only designed to accomplish your goals, but to shift your thinking. And then, your behavior changes and you will naturally do what will be the right thing for you. It seems magical!

The coaching process is particularly effective for emotional eaters, because it's very empowering. And let's face it; if you've been fighting the diet war throughout your life, you don't think anything will work. It's natural to be skeptical. You may have seen a dietician (I did) and you've learned a lot about food, exercise and weight loss throughout the years, and still failed. You have the solutions, and you know what you should do. But there's a missing link between what you know and what you do. That's the success of all my programs ~ I guide you using successfully researched strategies and you transform yourself.

And as you feel more and more empowered and in control, it's a natural choice to take care of yourself and develop a healthy relationship with food. Perhaps you can relate to Cheryl.

Cheryl was a 52yr old woman who had been dieting since she was a teenager. She was the youngest of 3 girls in a very athletic family, and although it was never said to her directly, she believed that she was 'fat'. Her mother and sisters were concerned about putting on weight, and Cheryl became conscientious about restricting herself too. Occasionally, she'd go on a strict diet and become very thin, but she could never maintain it. As soon as she broke her diet, the weight came back and the cycle would begin once again.

Losing weight consumed her thoughts. How well she ate the previous day, affected her mood and her entire disposition. And, regardless of how much she achieved in her life, she felt as if she was a failure. Cheryl continuously battled with herself. She was frustrated, and couldn't understand how the intelligent person she was, could be so weak and have 'no will power'.

Many emotional eaters feel that they are out of control, or 'not normal', because they know their behavior is unlike other people. They may eat secretly, when no one is looking, binge eat, wake up during the night and raid the fridge, or sabotage themselves in other ways, that make them feel guilty. This loss of control and failing at weight-loss, impacts their confidence and self-esteem in other aspects of their lives. It can contribute to inhibiting them from asking for salary increases, discovering new opportunities, participating in sports, or the simple joys in life.

Each of my coaching session starts with a topic that is not only informative, but alters your awareness and empowers you to make changes. Because we also learn by doing, there are homework assignments that encourage and support you along the way. In the first week, Cheryl and I discussed her beliefs and the perceptions she had about weight.

Much of our beliefs are created by what we see and hear through the media, our peers, family and the society. We internalize these beliefs and react accordingly. These theories are often unrealistic and unfounded, but they are powerful messages.

Cheryl's underlying belief was 'I am not good enough' unless I lose weight. But although she knew this was not true, that simple underlying belief was holding her back. Through the weekly assignments, Cheryl realized how much her older sister's casual remarks were the basis of many of her insecurities. And that these innocent childhood jibes had affected her food issues throughout her life. She discovered that although she was 52yrs of age, when these emotions were triggered, she resorted to eating 'bad food', just as she had done as a child.

Food addicts are 'hard wired' to crave something to eat, much like an alcoholic will desire a drink when they're under emotional stress. Smells, tastes and childhood foods evoke soothing memories, of comfort and safety. Places like watching TV, a vending machine, or the golden arches of MacDonald's can bring on cravings, that can be hard to resist. Stress, frustration, loneliness can also spark triggers and cravings, but as we worked through the coaching process and homework assignments, Cheryl learned to identify her triggers, handle her feelings, and use the new strategies without needing to resort to food.

In 6 weeks, Cheryl's perception of weight and the concept of what she 'should or 'should not' eat began to change. She realized that the demands she made on herself, contributed to her cravings, and the more she tried to resist, the worse they became until she finally gave in. She had fewer 'bad days', resulting in her being more optimistic, and her relationships with friends, family and coworkers improved as a result. As Cheryl now had techniques to loosen the restraints on what she ate, the dark cloud of feeling like a 'failure' lifted. This breakthrough empowered her so much that she now felt she was capable and deserved more out of life.

The new confidence had a snowballing effect. It inspired her to achieve a job promotion and become an active member at a gym. And as we worked together, she lost interest in controlling her weight and chose to adopt and maintain healthy eating habits. Healthy eating became a choice. And to her surprise, when she stopped obsessing about dieting, the excess pounds dropped off.

As impossible as this may seem, Cheryl's story is not uncommon. We have been trained to make demands on ourselves. We tell ourselves 'no pain, no gain'; that dieting should have rules and we should be disciplined and adhere to them. But, for an emotional eater, this advice works in reverse. When an emotional eater experiences pressure, it adds to their anxiety and eating is the only recourse they have to break the tension. Other dieters can lose a few pounds, stop dieting, and go back to eating normally, but to an emotional eater it's "all or nothing thinking". When they slip up on their diet, they need strategies to save them, or all their weight loss efforts will be abandoned. They'll feel guilty and depressed or 'start tomorrow', and their behavior will repeat as they soldier on.

I believe that the results and strength that you wish for is inside of you. And, I know that with the right environment, guidance and support, you can grow to be who you are meant to be physically, personally or professionally.

After almost 3 decades of coaching clients to make lasting life changes, I understand that what you need is not only knowledge, but a change in personal growth, which requires a shift in your thinking. What life coaching gives to my clients, is not only the ability to reach their goals, but to experience new heights, while gaining their life back. I feel very privileged to have the ability to witness these results.

About the Author

Beverley Glazer MA., CCC, ICCAC
Health & Wellness Coach
Change Agent

Beverley Glazer/ Coach/Counselor/Therapist/Motivational Speaker and Entrepreneur, has helped 1000s of women, over the past 27 years to overcome emotional eating, achieve new possibilities and ignite magic into their personal and professional lives.

Her clients stem from all walks of life: professional, non-professional, working, retired or those who never worked at all. The single commonality is that they feel stuck in one or more areas of their lives and they long for something to change.

As an experienced therapist, she has integrated proven researched techniques into her all her coaching, which guarantees you the results you wish for, in a minimum amount of time. Each session is designed to optimize your inner strengths and empower you – and have fun along the journey.

While holding a BA in Psychology (honors) MA in Counselling Psychology and certifications in Addiction, Gambling, Food, Sex, Relationships and Coaching, her personal experiences and the success she has achieved with her office clients, propelled her to help more people through online groups and 1 x 1 coaching.

'What you believe, you can achieve!'-*Mary Kay Ash*

I believe that you are never too old, and it's never too late to achieve the magic of becoming what you wish for. It would be my greatest pleasure is to support you through your journey.

Contact me privately to set up a time to chat and I'll answer all your questions and concerns.

Bev@ReinventImpossible.com
www.reinventImpossible.com/contact

Free Download: How To Beat Food Addiction Forever
https://bit.ly/2KX2kas

Programs: From Fat To Freedom
            Discover Yourself

Specialties: Empowerment & Self-Esteem, Personal Growth, Weight Loss, Mental Wellness, Health Coaching, Recovery Coaching, General Life Coaching, Finding Purpose, Life Transitions

"Jumping In With Both Feet: How Retreats Offer Powerful Transformation"

By Bronwyn Radcliffe, FNP, MSN, BSN, FMCHWC

With apprehension and regret, I turned off my phone and dropped it into the phone box; to be retrieved on Sunday afternoon. Hmm, how will I survive 5 days without a text, emails or phone call? "Disconnect to reconnect," the brochure said. It sounded good, no one to bother me for 5 days. But who will I be without my cell phone! If I don't fit in, what will I do? There's no place to hide. Glad I brought a book.

Retreats, from the Latin verb, "to pull back", have been a part of human life for thousands of years. The Christian retreat was popularized by St. Ignacius of Loyola in the 14th century to learn Spiritual Exercises. Meditative retreats are an important part of Sufism, while spiritual retreats are considered an essential component of Buddhism. Today retreats take on many different forms: solitary, community, silent, conversational, and educational. (11)

As I make my way out to the warm, sunny deck, I smile at a woman who seems just as uncertain as I. We sit together sipping a delicious concoction of ginger, basil and lime over ice, discussing just how challenging disconnection is going to be. We find some humor in it and move on to what brought us here. For me, I tell her about my exhaustion, my insomnia, and how I struggle to go to work. As a family nurse practitioner, I dread Monday's. I feel overwhelmed by all the patients needs, the pill for an ill mentality, how the EHR distracts from patient care, how patients never seem to get well. I'm exhausted all week, feeling a small surge of energy as the weekend rolls around.

But despite this, I have little energy or even desire to do much of anything. Family needs and time together feel like demands. I just want to escape. Even getting together with friends feels like effort. Liz tells me she is here for similar reasons. She is a corporate lawyer, working 50 hour weeks, over burdened by increasing demands at work and home. She tells me how the projects never seem to end. They scream "urgent" and come with unreasonable deadlines. And, to really make her life complicated, her mother, dealing with leukemia, is staying with her while she receives her chemotherapy. Like me, Liz is exhausted, mentally, physically, emotionally and says, "I feel hopeless. I sure hope this retreat does as promised".

Retreats allow for reflection, prayer, and meditation and help individuals and groups look at life, situations and issues from a different viewpoint. Removed from the usual routine and location of life, retreats allow one to focus all their attention on something they love, that which needs attention. This new perspective re-energizes and stimulates inspiration, breathing newness into life. Stepping out of the day to day routine creates space and time. And this space gives rise to awareness, genius and inspiration. Retreats support listening and giving space to really hear oneself, while detoxifying the stress and strain of the world. Deep relaxation is a result as one cleans out physically, mentally, emotionally. During this process one may see the truth of who they are. Finding time to pull back from life is essential to maintain whole health. (1,5,9)

A little bell rings and Bronwyn asks us all to gather in a circle. She begins with a simple, calming meditation and then we move to introductions, discuss the importance of this small group, confidentiality, respect and the importance of "showing up". I am not quite sure what that means, but since I'm here at the retreat, I'm gonna show up!

The morning moves quickly. Before I know it we are hiking in the woods. The views, the sense of awe, the serenity of the woods and the giddiness of being outside, in the sunshine is, well, intoxicating. I already feel freer, a little lighter. A smile creeps onto my face.

A study on the ancient Japanese meditative form of Nature bathing or Shinrin-yoku, showed that people who simply walked through a forest for two hours a day had lower concentrations of cortisol (the stress hormone), lower blood pressure and lower pulse rates. The study found that being outdoors boosted the levels of white blood cells, and anticancer proteins, and that even a one-day trip to a park can boost immune activity for at least a week. Another study published in *Environment and Behavior* showed that simply seeing trees reduced blood pressure and cortisol levels. Looking at, and being around the real thing has an even greater effect on the body, brain and mind. (6,8)

I've never been on a retreat before. I'm not really sure why I choose this, except I felt a deep need to get away. And, this one was highly recommended. An added bonus is work paid for it since I can get continuing education credits for it. The education part, how the stress response effects the mind and body, ways to mitigate it, how nature restores, how food is medicine, is all new to me. I've heard snippets in the news. I just started reading The Washington Post and The Huffington Post online and I've seen a few articles related to mind and body connections. So, I was intrigued. I've got to do something; I feel trapped, stuck, like there's no way out and nowhere to go. I feel like something is missing.

Meditation, from the Latin verb "to take the measure of" is a mental exercise of deep thought, contemplation. There are three basic types of meditation: concentrative, mindfulness and expressive. Research around meditation shows consistent daily practice provides powerful physical, mental and emotional changes that are sustained over time. Such benefits include reduction of blood pressure, blood sugar, depressive thoughts, and anxious behavior; an increase in immunity, circulation, and sleep, as well as focus, concentration, and cognitive function.

Studies using MRI show that long-term meditators have increased thickness in areas of the brain associated with attention, emotions and awareness of sensations. Meditators can literally change their brain, control their nervous system, increase their immunity and have better more restful sleep. And all this leads to you functioning better, remaining calm, in stressful situations. (3,8)

During free time on the first day we select the tent we wish to sleep in and spend some time settling in. I unfurl my sleeping bag and select a pad to put under it. Since tents are shared, Liz and I decide to room together. We decorate the inside with a couple of extra blankets and a few throw pillows. I put the flashlight right next to the door. It feels homey. I think I can do this. It's been years since I camped, but here it feels safe, despite being at the edge of a beautiful forest. The house is only a few yards away with indoor plumbing. "Glamping" is good!

Meals are a joint effort. At lunch one day we all pitched in to create a Thai Beef Salad. Greens from the garden, locally grown cherry tomatoes, cucumber, and shallots with seasoned local beef. It was so simple and delicious. Community cooking is part of the program. In an effort to teach us how to eat simply, organically, and locally, we collaboratively create the meals on the menu. Initially, I thought, I don't want to cook while restoring, but I have to say, cooking with 11 other women is fun! We laugh and joke and learn all about the foods we are preparing. Some cooking tips are offered and we all share what we know, blending our knowledge for the collective good.

Three evenings, over the course of these 5 days, we have a guest chef. Not only a great cook, he is funny, and its so obvious he loves to teach as he cooks. I never thought much about my food, where it came from or why I was eating it. A new awareness dawns as I notice that I feel light after meals, not heavy. I have energy like I haven't experience in years (and I am regular with my elimination, something else I needed).

Community Retreats offer the stimulation of connection. Humans are wired to survive and thrive; to grow personally, to connect. Connection, being with others, supporting, guiding and loving are some of the joys of being human. At retreats, a synergy takes place where all participants are exposed to a vast ocean of spiritual nourishment that helps everyone grow.

People who have had a profound spiritual experience have momentarily touched nirvana, and have been exposed to a tremendous surge of mindfulness energy. They are instantly transported to a higher level of consciousness, and are forever changed by what they see during those few moments of enlightenment. This is more likely to occur in a group setting. Personal growth and development occurs more rapidly at retreat or community settings than doing the work on your own.

The retreat format immerses us in a community of like-minded individuals, coming together for shared purpose. Retreats are powerful and potent.(1,3,8,9)

Each day seems to move quickly and yet time stands still. I can't explain it. It's already day 4 and I'm happier, feeling more relaxed than I have in years. Initially resistant to sleeping outside, I have never slept better. I am rested, waking refreshed, ready to go.

Increasing natural light exposure supports natural circadian rhythms. A study on camping showed that after a week-long camping trip in Colorado, without smartphones or even flash lights, circadian rhythms were reset. Study participants were ready for bed 2 hours earlier than their usual 12 am bedtime. They reported sleeping better, were more rested and had significantly less stress.

Several studies show fresh air improves the brain and body functions. The human brain uses the majority of the oxygen inhaled. So good quality oxygen is the best choice and the freshest air is outside. Sleeping in it, improves ones ability to think and process new ideas. Fresh air also breaks down lactic acid better than stale air. Air-conditioned homes and offices have larger amounts of carbon dioxide so lethargy is more common. Higher amounts of CO2 also increase anxiety.

Sleeping outside, listening to the sounds of nature, reduces stress levels and calms the mind. When stress is reduced cortisol levels drop, and that creates an increase in the body's immunity. The human body works best in parasympathetic (relaxation) mode. A study by Brigham and Women's Hospital and Harvard Medical School in Boston found that exposure to indoor fluorescent lighting prior to bedtime has a negative effect on sleep quality. It suppresses the production of the hormone melatonin, which regulates sleep and wakefulness, and in turn can effect "the body's ability to regulate body temperature, blood pressure and glucose levels".(4,12)

I really started to let go around the fire circle. We danced! It started with shaking. Ecstatic Dance, Bronwyn called it. We shook for 30 minutes, but it felt like 5. My mind flooded with old memories as I shook. They popped into my mind and, as instructed, I just let them come and watched them go. Then we paused, froze actually, and I felt...the movement of emotion, the flow of energy, the stillness of the night and my mind. And then we danced, allowing the body to move to the rhythm of the music, no rules, no one to judge, except myself. I felt so light and free after the dance circle. I had no idea that shaking could dislodge so much "stuckness".

David Fink, *Release From Nervous Tension*, J. Tripodi, *Freedom From Body Memory*, and B. Keeney *Shaking Medicine* all explain how emotion and trauma gets stuck in the body, the tissues, muscles, and cells, causing anxiety, depression and post traumatic stress. How we initially respond to a trauma informs the body for each successive trauma. Anxiety is our fear that we will experience the same trauma again, while depression is the holding of the emotion, sticking it deep down, not dealing with it.

Meditation can bring awareness to our responses, our intense concern as well as our ignored emotions. Research discusses how shaking, specifically creating tremor in the body, followed by deep relaxation, allows trauma to move out of the body. Shaking, pausing and then dancing dislodges, provides space for awareness, and finally reintegrates the nervous system to complete the release of trauma held in the body. (2,7,10)

Another favorite technique I learned was breathing. It sounds so basic, we do it all the time, but I had no idea there were so many different ways to breathe and that each way could make me feel differently. It was interesting to note that most of us were learning "how to breathe" for the first time. In general people breathe short, shallow breaths, and this type of breathing creates anxiety as carbon dioxide gets trapped in the lungs. It's the full removal of CO2, through a long exhale, that makes us feel light and more energetic. We practiced it and then compared it to other types of breathing. "Deep Belly" Breathing calmed me immediately. And the "Chaotic" breathing! Whoa, such clarity. I can't wait to take this back to my patients. It will help them as much as it's helped me.
As to the "showing up", I now know that means, emotionally being in the moment. And, I'm not good at it. This week brought many

awarenesses; I have to really practice showing up. When I breathe and calm myself, I find I can step out of my need, and be present for others. Being present I can "hear, see, know". It feels good to "show up" even though it's difficult. When I am present, when I show up, time stands still. And whatever I need is there for me (and the patient/client). The work gets done without effort. We practiced this all week in our group; active listening, really hearing the speaker and noticing how and what we were feeling as the speaker talked. I have had to learn to put away my response, so I can listen, really listen. I'll keep practicing this for me, my family and for my patients. And, eventually I will be able to teach them as well.

As this week draws to a close, I want to stay, but I am ready to go home. This retreat, this place, feels like home. I feel renewed, centered, like I can handle whatever comes my way. The skills I have learned here are so easy to use and easy to implement in the office and at home. I learned how to meditate, self calm, and bring mindfulness into my life, so I can establish a calm center, and show up. I learned about the limiting beliefs that hold me hostage and the constant borage of negative self-talk that flows through my head. I know I want to practice meditation daily. It feels really good and I haven't felt so alive in years.

I've learned how supportive and restorative nature is, how she softens the mind and eases the tension right out of my body. I may even sleep outside this summer! I've rediscovered my values, my character strengths and how those support me so I can live a purposeful life. And finally I've learned how to hear my intuition, how to accept it without criticism, and this allows me to move through life on my terms. Had I tried to learn all this on my own, it would've taken me years. The retreat immersed me into a sacred space with guidance and support to learn the language of me. I can't wait to do it again!

Research shows that people who attend meditation retreats leave the retreat with a greater sense of awareness. They are able to think more clearly, see reality at a deeper level and have greater control over their mind, body and emotions.(9,11)

I've packed my bags, given everyone a hug, grabbed a 'superhero muffin' to go and now I pick up my phone from the phone box. So reluctant to give it up only 5 days ago, now I don't want it. It's an intrusion in my life. It knocks me out of presence with its nagging texts, FB alerts and incessant emails. I don't think I'll turn it on until I get home. I know it's time to limit social media to once a week. I will join Bronwyn's Facebook group, where I can obtain support for loving me and maintain my resilience. I may even sign up for another retreat!

References

1. Dembling, S. 5 Reasons why a retreat is good for your business. Entrepreneur.
   https://www.entrepreneur.com/article/231195
2. Fink, D. Release from nervous tension. reprint 2011. La Vergne, TN
3. Francis, C.A. Mindfulness meditation made simple: Your guide to finding true inner peace. Paradigm Press. Raleigh, NC. 2014.
4. Hendrick, B. Light exposure may cut production of melatonin. WebMD Archives.
5. Hernandez, M.S. 9 Business owners reveal how retreats benefit their business.
   https://mshannonhernandez.com/how-retreats-benefit-your-business/
6. Jiang, B., Li,D., Larsen, L., et al. A dose response curve describing the relationship between urban tree cover density and self reported stress recovery.2014.
   https://doi.org/10.1177%2F0013916514552321.
7. Keeney, B. Shaking Medicine: The healing power of ecstatic movement. 2007. Destiny Books. Rochester, VT.
8. Park, B.J., Tsunetsugu, Y., Kasetani, T., Kagawa, T., Miyazaki, Y. The physiological effects of Shinrin-yoku

(taking in the forest atmosphere or forest bathing): evidence from field experiments in 24 forests across Japan. Environ Health Prev Med. 2010 Jan; 15 (1):18-26. doi: 10.1007/s12199-009-0086-9.

9. Throne, A. 7 Reasons you should consider retreats over a regular vacation. The Chopra Center. Blog.

10. Tripodi, J.A. Freedom from body memory: The courage to let go of the past and live creatively. 2009. Three Feet Productions. VA Beach, VA.

11. Wiki. https://en.wikipedia.org/wiki/Retreat_(spiritual)

12. Wright, K.P., McHill, A.W., Birks, B.R., et al. Entrainment of the human circadian clock to the natural lights-dark cycle. Current Biology. Vol. 23, Issue 16. P1554-1558, AUGUST 19, 2013. https://doi.org/10.1016/j.cub.2013.06.039.

About the Author

Bronwyn Radcliffe, FNP, MSN, BSN, FMCHWC

1998   Bachelor of Science in Nursing; Medical College of Virginia

2001   Masters of Science in Nursing; Virginia Commonwealth University

2001   Post Graduate certification as Family Nurse Practitioner

2008   Diplomat Anti-Aging and Functional Medicine American Academy of Anti-Aging Medicine

2017   Certificated Mind-Body Medicine Instructor   Center for Mind-Body Medicine

2017   Certified Functional Medicine Health & Wellness Coach Functional Medicine   Coaching Academy

2018   Bronwyn has an online coaching practice where she focuses on helping service professionals find clarity of purpose so they can live a life that supports a healthy, balanced lifestyle.

Ms. Radcliffe runs 5-day retreats throughout the year. Locations and outdoor excursions change depending on the time of year. All retreats teach mind-body skills, values, character strengths, positivity, and focus on self-love, self-awareness and self care. Retreats at Carly's Place also include cooking, food as medicine and sleeping outdoors.

Bronwyn offers a 10-week online "do it yourself" program that includes weekly online group coaching. For more information or to receive a free consult go to http://www.myInsightMBS.com.

When not coaching or teaching, Bronwyn, husband Reed and dog Carly spend time outside, biking, skiing, hiking, or backpacking the Rocky Mountains. Bronwyn enjoys creative sewing, adventure cooking, traveling, and reading. Bronwyn is the proud mother of four lovely, self-sufficient, grown children leading healthy, productive lives.

"Client Empowerment and Coaching for Results"

By Don L. Morgan, Ph.D.

As Simon Sinek says, "Start with your *why*."

This chapter author's *why*: I feel good when I can play a part in the success of others. I wrote this chapter to empower readers to venture out of their comfort zones and into the risky arena of opportunity. I hope this book will complement your decision-making and inspire action as you work to create the life you want.

Do you want a better life? Are you willing to experience the discomfort of trying new things that feel awkward and may not work very well at first? Of your existing activities, which ones are you going to put on your *Don't Do List* to create the life you want?

To intentionally create a better future, your *why* is largely determined by your mindset. The first part of this chapter deals with the basis of your *why* and how your mindset gives shape to that *why*. The second part of this chapter deals with why you may need a professional coach. Part 3 is about how a coach helps clients get positive results.

Part 1: The Life You Want Is Shaped by Your Mindset

Mindsets are beliefs about the permanence of your intelligence, your talents, and your personality. The concept was discovered by Stanford University psychologist Carol Dweck in decades of research on achievement and success. This section is based on Dweck's *Mindset: The New Psychology of Success* (www.mindsetonline.com).

Carol Dweck demonstrated that individuals can be classified on a continuum according to their implicit views of where their ability comes from. Some people believe their success is based on innate ability, holding to a "fixed" theory of intelligence. Others believe their success is based on hard work and learning—a "growth" mindset. Although we are unaware of our own mindset, we can discover it by our reactions to failure. This simple idea makes a huge difference. Our mindsets play an important role in all aspects of our lives.

Your view of life affects the way you shape your life. It can determine whether you become the person you want to be and whether you accomplish the things you value. Your mindset (fixed or growth), affects your choices, perspectives, and resulting achievements.

Every person sees and thinks differently. In that way, each person is unique. What you believe about yourself saturates every part of your life. From first grade through college, most people believe that perfection is the goal, and they focus on identifying and punishing their mistakes. Schooling tends to promote a fixed mindset.

Praise Versus Encouragement

Praise tends to keep students dependent on the approval of other people. Encouragement allows students to internalize their own actions. Children given praise such as "Good job, you're very smart" are much more likely to develop a fixed mindset. Encouragement such as, "You worked very hard and your work paid off" tends to produce a growth mindset.

For in-depth understanding, read Carol Dweck's book *Mindset*. She explains how:

- Brains and talent don't bring success; they stand in the way of it.
- Praising brains and talent doesn't foster self-esteem or accomplishment but jeopardizes them.
- Teaching a simple idea about the brain raises grades and productivity.

Fixed Mindset

People with a fixed mindset dread failure because it is a negative statement about their ability. They worry about their traits and how adequate they are. They have something to prove to themselves and others. People with the *fixed mindset* are driven to prove themselves in their careers and in their relationships. Their overriding concerns are: *Will I be accepted or rejected? Will I feel like a winner or a loser?*

The fixed mindset brings a consuming urgency to prove oneself over and over. Every situation calls for a confirmation of one's intelligence, personality, or character. Every situation carries a secret worry: Will I succeed or fail? Will I look smart or dumb? Will I be accepted or rejected? Will I feel like a winner or a loser?

Clients with a fixed mindset believe that their traits are permanent—nothing can change that. People in this mindset hide their weaknesses. They believe that their basic qualities of intelligence and talent are fixed traits. They work to document their abilities rather than develop them. They see talent as the key to success rather than effort.

Growth Mindset

Your true potential is unknowable. You cannot predict what you could accomplish with effort. As Dweck pointed out, "Darwin and Tolstoy were considered ordinary children; Ben Hogan was completely uncoordinated and graceless as a child; Geraldine Page, one of our greatest actresses, was advised to give up acting for lack of talent."

The growth mindset views the hand you're dealt as only the starting point for development. It is based on the belief that one's basic qualities can be developed by effort. Everyone can change and grow through application and experience.

Growth-mindset individuals accept failure because they realize their performance can be improved. The growth mindset allows people to live less stressful and more successful lives. These individuals are more likely to persist despite setbacks.

Again, clients with a growth mindset see their qualities as things that can be developed through dedication and effort. For example, while coaching basketball players about shooting free-throws, I didn't want them to feel bad about missing a shot. What they were instructed to do was to say to themselves, "Use more leg spring" or "Aim a bit more to the left" or "Use a higher trajectory" or whatever they learned from the missed shot. I wanted the players to believe that they could get better by choosing a positive reaction to failed attempts—in shooting basketballs and in life.

Clients with a growth mindset believe that their abilities can be developed through hard work—brains and talent are just the starting point. This perspective creates resilience that is essential for greatness. By shifting into a growth mindset, clients release pent-up motivation and increase productivity in all areas of life—business, education, sports, and relationships.

Mindsets change the meaning of failure. You are not a failure until you start blaming yourself. Coaches help you learn from your mistakes. Ironically, sticking to a job when it's not going well is the hallmark of the growth mindset. This mindset allows people to thrive during challenging times. Mindsets are just beliefs. A coach can help you see outcomes differently. You have a choice.

> **Creating the life you want is about learning,**
> **Not about demonstrating how smart you are.**

You might fool yourself by feeling smarter when you do something perfectly. The real progress is learning when you make mistakes. Effort expands your ability and turns it into accomplishment. Visit mindsetonline.com to learn more about this valuable concept.

The following section explains why you need a professional coach to help you create the life that you want.

Part 2: Why You Need a Professional Coach

To change the trajectory of your life, it helps to involve another person. Not just any person will do. You need one who is willing to put their own interests aside and tap into your goals and aspirations. You need a skilled professional coach.

Coaching is food for your mind. It is a smorgasbord of ideas and opinions. Are you searching for options and ideas? By phone, text, or in person, your coach will guide you to view issues from several vantage points.

Coaching facilitates building and maintaining your vital relationships. A professional coach will help you see the steps to reaching your goals. You may need someone to show you something that you didn't see by yourself. Your Personal Coach provides an opportunity to explore, to experiment, and to learn new ways of seeing and working. In crisis, the one to call is your Personal Coach!

Do you need a professional partner to help you work for a promotion, for a new job, or for success? Coaching that only shores up your self-esteem does not challenge you to grow. It may feel comfortable, but it does little to create the life you want. A professional coach will linger in the curiosity arena long enough to see your world. A coach is like a mirror for you to see how you get in your own way. This helps you see habit patterns that are holding you back. Then you will gain insight, confidence, and courage to act. It is a coaching mistake to get into strategies and fixes prior to seeing things from the client's view. Premature specification gets in the way of creating a satisfying life.

Coping activities such as TV binge watching, reading, shopping, and overeating can get in the way of growth. Coaching brings attention to Past–Present–Future. Where have you been, where are you now, and where are you going? Short-term fixes can sabotage long-range goals. Coaching helps clients see unanticipated outcomes of anticipated action. What do you want? What will get you there? What will that achievement get you?

Personal empowerment is about finding your untapped talents. It becomes a framework for your Big Dream Goals. Coaching can help you make smarter decisions, focus on priorities, and deal more effectively with frustration and chaos. Coaching provides self-confidence, clarity, growth mindset, and wellbeing.

Purposeful engagement is the key to unlocking your human potential. Coaching can help you stay on track and hold you accountable. Coaching reduces the tendency to procrastinate. For example, New Year's resolutions have a much higher success rate when such commitments are declared to a coach. As clients contemplate upcoming coaching sessions, their thoughts intensify the desire to fulfill commitments made during previous sessions. Anticipation and expectation drive behavior.

The result is that coaching provides a safe place to vent and to break through barriers. Candor is the key to progress.

Part 3: How a Coach Helps Clients Get Positive Results

Curiosity is the primary coaching tool. It gives the coach super power for engineering client change. This involves excavating client potential, values, and image of the client's ideal life. Action items come to the surface and emerge through this process. Coaching Functions include:

- Listening to Dreams, Disappointments & Challenges.
- Clarifying Priorities, Limits, Options & Outcomes.
- Inquiring by asking about Purpose, Goals & Achievements.
- Mentoring: Growth Mindset, Effective Communication & Relationship Skills.
- Talent, trait, and skill assessing.
- Reflecting client statements to add clarity.

The coach is an agent of change to confront issues and to help clients tolerate the discomfort that accompanies change. With your coach, you can practice new behaviors in a safe and accepting environment. Effective coaching encourages clients to persist despite failure.

When coaching, it's natural to want to give the best that we have to our clients. It's more important to provide what the client needs, not what the client wants. Focus on what the client needs to create a better life. A coach is more effective by providing the content to fill in the gaps that will promote a balance in the client's perspective and thinking.

As an example, think about a head football coach. He must take charge, give orders, make decisions, and see that they are carried out. In personal coaching the tables are turned. The client becomes the decision-maker. The coach's role is to provide inspiration, support and clarification. That may involve taking a role in the relationship that is outside the coach's comfort zone. The DiSC System, explained in the next section, provides a way to illustrate situational role-taking.

Situational Role-Taking for Effective Coaching

To improve coaching effectiveness, it helps for the coach to take on the most appropriate role for the situation. I use DiSC terms as an easy way to describe Situational Coaching. "D" stands for Dominance, "i" stands for inspiration, "S" stands for Support, and "C" stands for Correctness. The DiSC System was developed by John Geier to classify behavior styles and tendencies. (The lower case "i" in DiSC was first used for clarification and not be confused with "L" or "1". Later, use of the small "i" became a branding item.)

During much of the situational coaching process the coach interacts with the client in a manor that induces the "D" role in the client—making decisions and commitments. The coach will switch from one role to another role, as necessary to promote positive growth of the client. A simplified description of the roles taken by the coach are summarized below:

i-Role

Operating from the "i" role, the coach is spontaneous, enthusiastic and less concerned with details. The function is to provide positive emotion and inspiration—to inspire, to affirm, and to motivate. Coaches help clients see their accomplishments. It is a move from fear-based behavior (reaction) to a goal orientation behavior (action).

S-Role

Sometimes a client just needs to talk about something—not to get sympathy or advice—but to kill its power by allowing the truth of things to hit the air. Emotion distorts decision-making. An objective listener is vital. Professional coaches support their clients' drive for success by listening and asking clarifying questions. Reflective listening and clarifying questions facilitate insight and growth. Showing that you care provides understanding and empathy.

This role is most effective for working with upset and distraught clients. In such a situation, the coach appears easy-going and calm. The coach is a good listener and pays attention. She asks questions about specifics, is thoughtful, and thinks about things while withholding opinions. Taking this role provides the opportunity for clients to explore possible strategies and tactics before they implement them. They can rehearse and refine critical announcements in private with an objective and unbiased professional. Coaching is actually a client's personal laboratory for testing strategies, new ideas, and messages.

C-Role

Life is a marathon, not a sprint. It is easy to get caught up in immediate matters at the expense of more important long-term matters. In this role, the coach is cautious, asks many questions and carefully studies specifications and issues. The coach must consider the surroundings and environment, analyze problems, and look at issues thoroughly. The coach must follow regulations, spot unanticipated consequences, and offer suggestions based on fact, rather than opinion.

Coaching can minimize the effect of CEO disease or Group Think. These conditions occur when executives are surrounded by worshipers or when critics are exiled or when decisions favor short-term fixes rather than long-term growth.

In the C-Role, one tool used to provide structure is S-W-O-T. Here the client is asked about personal Strengths and Weaknesses, and about Opportunities and Threats. This brings to mind a client whose tendency is to focus on his strengths and opportunities and to disregard his weaknesses and possible threats. Knowing what specific questions to ask and knowing when to ask them is one key to successful coaching. SWOT is only one of hundreds of coaching tools available.

Talking about problems is typical. To facilitate positive growth, discuss successes and joyful times. A valuable coaching tool for instilling Growth Mindset — Appreciative Inquiry — is summarized below.

Appreciative Inquiry (AI) is an effective way for coaches to instill a growth mindset. AI was pioneered in the 1980s by David Cooperrider and Suresh Srivastva, two professors at the Weatherhead School of Management at Case Western Reserve University. AI consultants around the world are increasingly using an appreciative approach to bring about collaborative and strengths-based change in thousands of profit and nonprofit organizations and communities in more than 100 countries.

AI is a way of being and seeing. It is a process for facilitating positive change. The assumption is simple: Every person has something that works right–things that are vital, effective, and successful. AI begins by identifying this positive core and connecting to it in ways that heighten energy, sharpen vision, and inspire action for change.

AI can increase positive feelings and make generative thinking and positive action more likely. AI focuses on what's already working. To understand how to create the desired future, AI can teach you to approach a situation with a new perspective that considers all aspects with a positive, strengths-based focus. AI offers clients the opportunity to broaden their perspectives and create positive outcomes.

The 4 Stages of Appreciative Inquiry

To achieve a transformational change, AI protocol has four stages: Discovery, Dream, Design, and Destiny/Delivery.

1. Discovery

This process is designed to "discover and disclose one's positive capacity" e.g., to find, emphasize, and illuminate factors that have led to 'the best' in a given situation. You will look for peak experiences that touch your heart and see things in a new light. Strategically formulated coaching questions elicit positive stories, examples, and metaphors from clients. Questions that a coach might use about your daily life could be:

- What are the most significant stories in your life?
- What things are going well in your life?
- How are you making a difference?

2. Dream

Once you have discovered the best, then comes the Dream Stage. Dream of what could be or needs to be and challenge the status quo. Focus on the possibility of what could be rather than on the limiting ways people normally do/feel/see/act or react. Through this you will begin to see and understand things in a new way. This is where clients work to come up with a representation of their highest aspirations and dreams for their ideal future.

3. Design

Sharing discoveries and possibilities with your coach and using dialogue and debate will help you to decide on how to create the life you want. Identifying concrete actionable ideas will make your newly envisioned potential seem doable.

4. Destiny

This phase is more than acknowledging aspirations. It is where you commit to a plan of action.

Professional Coaching Specialties

There are hundreds of coaching niches in the Professional Life Coach field. Some of the specialties and certifications held by the author are listed below.

- Positive Psychology Practitioner
- Anger Management Facilitator
- Strengths, Personality, and Trait Assessment scales
- Leader Effectiveness Training Facilitator
- Conflict Management Consultant
- Couples Coach
- Parent Effectiveness Training
- Motivational Interviewing

In Conclusion

Top professionals in all areas have personal coaches. So can you! You have much more potential for brain development and ability for learning at any age than you realize. You can shape your temperament and skills through training, experience, and effort. Starting with a small step forward and continuing by taking one step after another, you will be empowered to create the life you want.

If no one laughs at your goals, they are not big enough!

The evidence is overwhelming that people can develop throughout their lives. One way is to spend time with people who challenge you. Look for pursuits that will stretch you. Striving to achieve stretch goals is the hallmark of the growth mindset. This perspective will set you up for success and give you the strength to thrive during challenging times.

When you look at your experiences through the growth-mindset-lens, you see the transformative power of your efforts. It robs you of all your excuses. It is within your power to choose to look at your experiences through the growth-mindset-lens and to choose to work hardest for the things you love the most. You have a choice. Your coach can help you build or strengthen your growth mindset and create the life you want.

About the Author

Don L. Morgan, PhD, Positive Psychology Practitioner and Professional Coach, holds certificates in a number of areas, including Leader Effectiveness Training, Executive Coach, Master Life Coach, Master Business Coach, Motivational Interviewing, and Law of Attraction Practitioner. Morgan was certified by John Geier as a Performax Phase III Consultant on August 21, 1981. He has participated in all five World Congress of Positive Psychology conferences held every two years.

After graduating from high school and from college in the lower third of his classes, he decided to continue his education as far as he could, not expecting to earn a graduate degree. He wasn't going to quit until the school stopped him. For his Master's Degree, he earned a B+ average. After his first year at the University of Iowa he received an academic scholarship, and an assistantship,

Don started his professional career as an athletic coach and social studies teacher in Melba, Idaho. After 4 years of coaching and teaching, Don worked for a year as a marketing consultant for a Denver company. Then he went back into the education business. After 6 years as a secondary teacher and coach, he moved into the principal's office at Amana (Iowa) High School. Two years later he accepted work as a consultant for the University of Iowa. Upon completion of his

Ph.D., Morgan joined the Research Learning Center at Clarion State College as Assistant Director for Field Services.

During his 31-year tenure at Clarion University, Professor Morgan served in a variety of positions including teaching professional practicum, supervising student teachers, operating an experimental school, teaching management classes, counseling, and the Director of Cooperative Education and Internships.

Morgan's work with the Positivity Academy involves coaching and training Positivity Coaches and Organizational Consultants. He thrives on seeing his clients achieve their goals.

> For every problem under the sun,
> There is a fix or there is none.
> If there be a fix, seek til you find it.
> If there is none, never mind it.

http://morganmanagementconsulting.com
http://www.positivityacademy.com/

Instagram: @positivityacademy

"Weekly Exercises to Expand Yourself and Your Client Base"

By Boni Oian

I have found the more I dig into what brings up my judgments about others, the more it allows me to transform judgments about myself. This process has expanded my happiness, joy and client base.

I am sharing these weekly exercises with you, so you too can expand your life and in the process create the life you want. Pick one exercise and stick with it for the whole week. If you find one too difficult, you can always repeat it.

1) Develop the accountability habit.
Hold yourself accountable for everything you say and do.

The best way to start this is to decide to start today. That means you are **not** going to look to your past and notice all the times you didn't do what you said you would.

Start with something simple. Make a list of the things you are going to do today. Then, do them and cross them off your list. They don't have to be big things, as your subconscious doesn't know the difference between big and small tasks. Each is just considered one thing.

Say out loud, "I am completing these things on my list today."

Put on your list:
- Brush your teeth.
- Have breakfast.

- Get dressed.

Do these three things, and then cross them off the list while feeling good about yourself. This is a great start!

2) Give less advice--and ask more questions.

Only offer advice after you ask if it's okay to give your opinion or experience.

Always start that information with, "I don't know what <u>you</u> need to do, but in my experience..." or "When I am faced with that situation, what usually works for me is..."

When someone asks my advice, usually they just want to tell me something they did and see if it matches what I can help them with. In that case, after they ask their question, I ask, "Why do you ask?" Now I can choose to offer information about the real issue.

Here's an example: Marcia calls me and asks, "What would you do if someone unfriended you on Facebook?" So I ask, "Has that happened to you?" Now the story comes out. Don't waste time thinking someone wants your opinion when they just want to open the door to tell their story. This way, they get what they want, and you don't have to run the risk of offending them with your point of view.

3) Care--about your health, your wealth, your wants and your personal development.

Most of us care about the people around us more than we care about ourselves. We might have been taught at an early age that it's "selfish" to care about ourselves, and that being selfish is bad.

Let's get rid of that notion right now. Being self-ish is being like ourselves. Who else are we expected to be? Or act like? Usually when others told us that, it was because they wanted us to make them look like a good parent or person. It didn't have anything to do with us.

So now, caring for or improving upon your health, wealth, education, skills and talents needs to be part of your personal daily goals.

Pick one thing you can do today to improve your:
- Health--eat a carrot.
- Wealth--put one dollar in a savings plan.
- Education--learn a new word in the dictionary.
- Skills--practice something you already do, like tennis, golf or the piano.
- Talents--sing or write or go to the next level in what you already do well.

Remember, one degree of change today can mean 10 degrees' shift by year's end.

4) Be a walking advertisement for self-respect.
How do you treat yourself in public as well as private? Do you put yourself down verbally when you make a mistake, stub your toe or drop something?

Think of someone you respect and notice anything they do differently than you do regarding how they treat their body, car or wardrobe.

In your life, how can you use the message of self-respect they give off by their actions?

My suggestion is that you start with one thing. Today, let's start by removing name calling from your vocabulary. Choose now never again to call yourself stupid, klutz, clumsy, idiot or _____. (You fill in the blank.)

5) Value yourself.

Value yourself and you will start to appreciate yourself. You may have been told to love your neighbor as yourself. Unfortunately, if we don't love ourselves, we can hardly love our neighbor. How do we love ourselves when we may not even like ourselves?

Start making a list of everything you think of yourself. Make this list in two columns. On one side put what you do like about yourself. In the other column, list what you don't like about yourself.

Now, on the "like" side, write the opposite trait of what you have on the "don't like" side. An example would be, if you have "disorganized" on your "don't like" list, place "organized" on your "like" side.

Here is your challenge. Read this **new** "like" list daily as if you already have all these traits.

Start with "I am" or "where am I" and continue to read down your list, adding as much enthusiasm as possible. Do this continually for 30 days and notice the changes in your life.

6) Be punctual as just one way to keep your agreements.

There are two fallouts with not keeping your agreements:
1. Other people don't believe what you say and therefore don't respect you.
2. You don't have any integrity with your word and don't respect yourself.

You can choose not to keep any agreements and just own that you are willing to be a liar, or you can start changing your automatic response to one of meaning what you say and doing what you promise.

7) Acknowledge yourself when you make progress or get things "right."
There are always days when you jump for joy and say, "I was meant to do this!"

Celebrating your successes tells your subconscious mind, "Yes! I want more of this." You can also let others celebrate your successes. Both actions may feel uncomfortable at first, but remember to breathe, keep your comments to yourself, and just say thank you. This takes practice.

Things happen when this practice gets comfortable:
- You feel better about yourself.
- You don't look to others to acknowledge you and therefore aren't disappointed because they don't.
- You start acknowledging others sincerely.
- All that acknowledgement starts catching on exponentially.
- You have just made your world a better place to live or you have pushed people's buttons for them to know what's up for clearing.

This week look for things to celebrate about what you do, what you don't do, how you think, and all small accomplishments. Start a way to remind yourself of all your celebrations at the end of the month.

You could:
- Save all your lists of your scratched-off items to review monthly or yearly.
- Put different-sized stars on your calendar for things completed.
- Put coins in a bank for a monthly blowout (pennies for brushing your teeth, nickels or quarters for waiting until after dinner for dessert).

Whatever works for you, do it and make it an exciting habit that you will want to keep.

8) Listen to what your feelings are telling you; trust them no matter what anyone says.
If we were taught to listen to our feelings as children, our authority issues would be minimal because we would own our own authority.

Guilt would not exist!

We wouldn't compare how we do things and how we think about things to the "experts." Also, we wouldn't feel the need to lie because we wouldn't feel that we would be judged or made wrong by telling our truth.

We are where we are, so let's start now by uncovering the places where we were taught to give our power away.

This week notice where you either tend to lie to people or want to lie to them. Make a list of who is involved and the circumstances or environment where it shows up. An example might be you feel like you want to lie to your dentist when you're in his office, but don't have the urge when you meet him in the grocery store.

Next, when the feeling of guilt shows up, ask yourself, "Who do you think would judge what you are doing?" It's not going to be everyone. It's your mom, dad or someone else. Once you have a person in mind, mentally explain to them that you are making your own choices now. Then, thank them for contributing to your life so you could get where you are today.

Now that you are more aware of your triggers, listen to your feelings and decide if you feel it's a good idea to continue your actions. This way you can start understanding your true feelings about your actions instead of the feelings of letting an outside authority down.

9) Do what you can, and that's good enough.
Waiting until you can do it perfectly and completely is a game we play when we don't want to put something out and be open to criticism. If you never put your work out to the world, you never have to hear that it isn't good enough or have to see it compared to someone else's work.

Being perfect isn't really about making it perfect; it's about the fear of feeling that old, uncomfortable feeling of being shamed or judged. Once you understand that someone else would always do it differently or have an opinion about how you need to do something, you can give up the perfect game.

This week, finish what you have been putting off and put it out to be seen.

Arm yourself with these statements and questions when you hear opinions and points of view:

- That's an interesting point of view.
- So how exactly did you do it?
- Why is it important to you to have it done that way?
- Can I see yours and how you did it?
- Would you buy it if I changed it that way?

Instead of standing there feeling slapped in the face, breathe into the feeling in your body and tell it like you would a small child: "It's okay, you're okay, I can protect you, I love you." If the feeling persists, tell it, "You did nothing wrong," and make a symbol of peace and love in the most comfortable color you can think of and send that symbol to where the feeling resides in your body.

10) Don't criticize or talk down to yourself.

If a friend came to you and told you their problems, would you criticize them for getting themselves into the situation or would you listen to the dilemma and offer kind, thoughtful suggestions?

It could be time to treat yourself like your very best friend, someone you have respect for and want to keep around.

- What would that look like to you?
- What would that feel like to you?
- Would you be willing to find out how many times in the day you put yourself down? Say something nice to yourself?

Carry a small notebook with you this week. Every time you think something degrading about yourself, write it down. If you stub your toe and say, "You idiot," write down where you are and what the circumstances around the event are.

If you complete a project and say, "Good job!" write down where you are and what the circumstances around that event are.

At the end of the week, take out your notebook and look for patterns. You may notice you criticize yourself when you make mistakes and other people are present. Or you praise yourself when you are by yourself.

Once you see your pattern, work on doing the opposite. Praise yourself when others are present or when you are in the company of an authority. Now notice if you feel comfortable or if you are waiting for the other person to say something.

As with all uncomfortable feelings, breathe, locate the feeling in your body, and send it a symbol of peace and love.

11) Don't lie, especially to yourself.

Let's look at why you would lie in the first place. Ask yourself, "Do I hold the person I am lying to in an authority position?"

Also, "Do I believe the person I am lying to will judge me?"

Usually, if you are lying to someone else, you hold them in an authority position, for instance a doctor, dentist, police officer, or boss. If you are lying to yourself, you are usually in judgment of your thoughts or actions.

Once trust is broken, it may never be mended. Are you really willing to risk that? What is the risk? That you will never be able to look that person in the eye again without feeling shame, guilt or some other unwanted feeling. They will probably feel that you are lying, and then they will question anything you say from now on.

The exercise this week is to notice and record anyone you lie to. Also, record any time you catch yourself justifying what you said or did. At the end of the week, pretend the other people, one at a time, are in front of you and say, "I'm sorry I said (fill in the blank). Please forgive me."

Where you were lying to yourself, look in a mirror and say, "You didn't do anything wrong. Someone taught you those thoughts were shameful. Thoughts are just thoughts."

Telling yourself the truth keeps you in present time, and present time is where you create your future. Choose now to accept all thoughts and to act only on the ones you want in your future.

12) Break things down into doable and realistic steps.
In accomplishing any project, the first thing is knowing where you are going. What does it look like, feel like or how will you know when you are finished?

Then, allow yourself to daydream about all the ways to accomplish it, knowing that these ideas come from the subconscious mind. The subconscious mind is a storehouse of information that you have seen or done before. Once that information comes to the surface, then you are ready for the unknown or inspired way.

Write down everything that comes to you. Look over your list and ask yourself, "What can I do right now?"

Act on the things you can do right now. Once completed, then ask the same question and act on those things.

Cross off the list as you go to create momentum by acknowledgement. It's not about getting to the destination or getting the project finished and then feeling good. It's about feeling good about yourself as you go.

This week follow this pattern for all you do and notice your enthusiasm for life's projects change.

13) Know your boundaries. Then don't cross them.
It really doesn't matter what others think of you. It just matters what you think of yourself.

If you set boundaries for yourself and then cross them, you might start thinking of yourself as wishy-washy, wimpy or as having no integrity.

As these thoughts take hold, your self-esteem will take a downward spiral. How far you let it go is up to you.

Now is decision time. Do you want to keep your old boundary or are you willing to set a new boundary? Sometimes looking at the old boundary you notice that:

- You have outgrown that boundary.
- It was never yours to start with, just one that was inherited.
- The same circumstances don't apply now as they did when you first made that boundary.

Make a promise to yourself that this week when you see yourself cross your own boundary, you will STOP, decide to keep it or list it as in one of the above categories and make a new boundary.

14) Replace the word "fail" with "correction" or "new challenge."
How would you feel differently at the end of the day if you said, "I found a new challenge to the project I'm working on," instead of "I failed at my project?"

Be willing to risk failure to make something new and different. Stretching yourself often requires new thinking, experimenting and corrections.

Be willing to give up the belief that failure is even part of the process. Replace the word failure with correction.

Think action – result – correction, action - result – correction until you acquire the result that best suits the situation.

Sometimes, you just run out of time, and the end result of where you are is good enough.

This week, practice saying, "Correction," with anything that needs attention. Also, allow yourself to say, "Good enough!" with projects you run out of time on.

15) Become a finder.

When you become a solution-seeker and finder of that solution, the hunt is far more exciting. What you hunt for, you will find, so why not hunt for where you are already perfect, right and loved?

Hunt for why you are good enough, why you are capable and why you are unlimited.

If you want, start a yearly journal and make your New Year's Eve celebration rereading everything and everywhere you achieved greatness.

Another way is to write on your calendar all your achievements throughout the year. Put at least five accomplishments in every calendar space. Even the simple things have meaning when they are acknowledged.

Remember, what you are saying is "What I do is important," therefore, "I am important." Then, watch your actions. Because you are acknowledging yourself, you will begin to acknowledge others more easily. Keep track of that, too.

16) Be specific instead of vague.

There is enough confusion in the world without your adding to it. How many times have you asked someone if they wanted to do something and they said, "I guess so." Now, do you know if they would really like to or not? An answer like "I guess so" leaves the interpretation up to the listener.

There is nothing wrong with being decisive and voicing your preference. If the person asking doesn't want your opinion, they probably won't ask.

Sometimes people do ask just so they can tell you what they think, but most the time, they just want to know your preferences a little better.

So, this week, say what you mean and mean what you say. Practice saying yes when you mean yes and no when you mean no. If you prefer blue over red, say so. Keep track and notice when you are less likely to be decisive. Who is it around? What is the subject? Do you really know what you want or do you have to think about your answer?

17) Don't assume.
Don't assume — ask for definitions of words that could mean different things to different people. Even people raised in the same family have different meanings for words.

"Why is that?" you ask? Because of the emotion attached to the word, for starters. Then you add how it was used in the environment and where the emphasis is placed, and you get a whole different connotation for the word.

Sweetie, baby, honey and cutie can be very endearing words or they could evoke a lawsuit or black eye. Same word, different setting, and totally different intention, as well as results.

This week monitor your words. Make a list of words you use that have different meanings, for example: Great, great, <u>great</u>. And that's before you add any other words to it like Oh. Oh, Great, Oh, great, Oh, <u>great.</u>

18) Mind your own business.

It's easy to see what others "should" do from our point of view. We must remember it is just "our point of view." It isn't necessarily what is best for someone else.

You don't know another's path or purpose, so don't get caught up in running their life. You have enough to handle running yours. If everyone would remember this, there would be no plots for sitcoms.

You can always offer your experience or opinion, just make sure you are invited to.

Sometimes people are afraid to ask other people's opinions, so you may ask, "Do you want to know what I think or what I might do in that case?" Find out clearly if your input is wanted before you input it.

Use this opportunity to look at your own life and ask these questions:

- Is there any area of my life that looks similar?
- How can I use, in my life, what I was going to suggest to them?
- What am I avoiding looking at in my life?
- What's not perfect yet in my life?

19) Ask directly for what you want, need or expect.

Expecting others to read your mind and act accordingly is just asking for disappointment and is a disservice to them and to yourself.

Most people aren't mind readers, and they are usually busy thinking about what **they** want. Mostly, people are afraid of rejection, so they don't ask for what they want.

Let's just get rid of the notion that if someone says no to your request, they are rejecting you. All they are doing is choosing not to do what you ask.

It could be they are saying no for a couple of reasons:
- They may not have what you are asking for.
- They may not have the time.
- They may not have the money or choose to spend it that way.
- There are many reasons, so don't think it's about you.

Ask for 3 things this week from different people. If they say no, tell them thank you for considering your request.

State clearly and honestly what you think and feel. This, at times, is hard for people who either don't know what they think and feel or who want to avoid thinking and feeling something different than the person they are talking to.

So, first start with something simple like stating, "I like chocolate. I feel indulgent when I eat it."

Now you can move on to more controversial subjects.

"I love that hair style. I feel like I fit in with my coworkers when I have my hair styled that way."

Keep practicing and soon you will be able to own both the way you think and the way you feel.

This week state at least once a day what you think and follow it up with what you feel.

20) Practice self-compassion and self-nurturing action.

Practice self-compassion and self-nurturing when you mess up or are feeling fragile. In other words, treat yourself as a friend. What would a friend do when someone is at their lowest?

They might offer a compassionate ear, give a gift of a massage or pedicure.

Remember, you are not superwoman all the time. There are times when you may feel invincible, and there are also times when you may feel very vulnerable or fragile. It's not a character flaw to be fragile. It's just one of the many feelings we hold.

Eliminate all name-calling to yourself. No more using words such as klutz, brain dead, idiot, worthless or _____ (fill in the blank).

Show yourself compassion once a day this week and learn by practicing enjoying the nurturing.

21) Be professional and ethical – always.

When you must justify your actions, you might want to look again at why you are doing them.

The rule of thumb is, if you can't do something with a clean conscience, don't do it.

Always ask yourself, "If I had to stand in front of an authority figure and admit what I did, would it feel comfortable?"

Even though you are your own authority, anyone else that you might want to lie to is still someone you hold as an authority over you. If you would lie to your dentist, CPA, doctor, God or your mother, you still hold them as being your authority.

It's time to take your power back. Do what you know to be right from your values.

Remember, you must live with yourself and your actions. If you repress them, they will resurface. You can try to hide them, but sooner or later they will be the secrets that run your life.

Do only what contributes to your consciousness and the consciousness of others.

22) Spend time getting to know yourself intimately.
You might be surprised to find out what a great person you are. You may also learn that you even like yourself.

To start, pretend you have just met this new person called YOU. Ask questions to find out what YOU like, dislike, enjoy as a hobby, value, enjoy as a favorite color or movie. Now you have some place to start to build a relationship with YOU.

Now, treat YOU as your best friend by hearing his/her fears, worries and dreams. Listen without judgment, criticism or skepticism. Listen as if the dreams could be realized.

Say, "I hear you," "I love you," and "I support you," as an answer to everything YOU say.

Notice how you feel at the end of the day!

23) Stand up for yourself when necessary.
If others want to knock you down, that's because of their fear. Be sure to let them know that you are not afraid. This can be

done with a simple, "I don't see it that way," if someone is putting you down or making fun of you.

Remember, gods don't need to be defended, and if we are all part of the divine source, or God, we don't have to defend ourselves.

Some people must belittle someone else to hide their insecure feelings. See this for what it is and speak directly to the insecure person underneath the bluster.

"Why does that bother you?" or "Does it really matter how I dance? "or "Maybe I just enjoy what I am doing," are all great answers that allow you to acknowledge the 'jab' and let them know it doesn't mean a thing to you.

Also, asking how they would do it, what their suggestion is, and how they have learned to complete the task at hand are great ways to give them what they are really wanting--the attention to be on them.

24) Be yourself.
Be yourself, as there is no one else on the planet that has had the exact same experiences, purpose, karma and desires.

You learn from others in all areas of your life; then, you put that to use in what you say and do in any given moment. This makes you unique in every way and in every moment.

You have a lot of memories to choose from as you decide which course of action to take. Again, this makes you unique in your relationships and how you conduct yourself.

The best exercise to do is, when the first response to a situation presents itself, wait, and then ask, "Is there a better way to handle this situation that will create a 'win' for everyone involved?"

See how many 'wins' you can accumulate this week! **Keeping track of wins allows you to acknowledge yourself.**

25) Only make promises you can keep.
Don't make promises unless you intend to deliver on them. Make yourself notes and, if you can't keep your promise, simply let people know as soon as possible.

Sometimes in the heat of the moment we agree to something in the future; then we forget all about it. The forgetting and therefore not doing the thing we promised is what keeps us from being in integrity with ourselves and others. Once you go back on your word about one thing, it's easy to go back on more things.

You get what you want, which is praise, when you say you'll do something or show up. Now the energy is gone, and you don't follow through. This has a lasting impression on the people you stand up, and it isn't a favorable one in their eyes.

This week make good on your all promises, especially the ones to yourself.

26) I don't know.
If you don't know – admit you don't know – and if you deem it important, make an effort to find out about the subject.

The worst thing you can do is talk around the issue, pretend you know but can't say, try to confuse people with double talk or change the subject. In other words, sound like a politician.

Some people will even go as far as raising their voices and getting opinionated about the subject rather than admit they don't know the facts.

What purpose does this serve? Do you really believe people don't see through this? What overall impression are you really making? Is this the impression you want people to have of you?
Asking these questions will make it easier for you to say, "I don't know." or "I'm not sure."

In today's world, you could even say, "My name isn't Mr. Google!"

27) Commitment
Get comfortable with commitment. If you can't commit, say so. Saying no is just as easy as saying yes when you practice.

If you are worried about hurting someone's feelings if you say no, think about how hurt they are going to be if they are counting on you and you let them down at the last minute.

It's better to say no. Then, if plans change, you can say yes, and have it well received. This way there is no obligation and you can choose in the moment.

You have the right to say no. You have the right to say yes. Practice saying what you truly mean this week and notice the response of others.

A friend of mine always says, "Yes, I will call you this week." She doesn't call, so now I don't believe anything she says. Is that how you want others to think of you? If no, learn to say no.

28) Don't try to impress.

BE yourself--that is impressive, rare, you will stand out, and people will know what to expect from you.

Being honest and present are the two most impressive things you can be.

Have you ever had someone look around, wave at others and just nod or say yes while you're talking to them? How does that make you feel? Mostly it makes people feel like what they are saying is not important and, therefore, they are not important.

If you want to make others feel special in your company then find an honest compliment you can think to yourself while they are talking.

Now, I have been around some negative people, and the best I could come up with was that their glasses set straight on their face. That's enough of a compliment to change the way you are thinking about someone and therefore change the 'vibe' you are giving off.

What you are thinking really does matter in the overall feeling of the situation and is felt by others whether they understand it or not. Then you might want to say the compliment out loud and see what happens.

In Conclusion

These weekly exercises can change the way you live your life and it only takes a few minutes a day to try some of them. I encourage you to see how they can help and it you need more support in accomplishing them, a life coach can help.

About the Author

Boni Oian - Life Navigator

Author of *Claim Your Life – Transform Your Unwanted Subconscious Beliefs into an Exhilarating Source of Power,* Boni trains people to instruct her Claim Your Life process worldwide.

She is certified by the International Medical and Dental Hypnotherapist Association and she's certified as a Catalyst Coach by the Ace Success Center and the International Association of Professional Life Coaches®.

Boni's certifications as an Akashic Record Teacher and Consultant are from Akashic Records Consultants International and Akashic Knowing School of Wisdom.

She is a ThetaHealing Instructor and Practitioner certified by Vianna Stibal's THInK and an Instant Miracle Practitioner by Christian Michelsen.

Boni focuses on training and consulting people, so they can enjoy living the life they want.

830.537.4523
www.ClaimYourLifewithBoni.com

Boni@ClaimYourLifewithBoni.com

Let's see if what we can do together. Schedule a free session at http://www.claimyourlifewithboni.com/theta-healing-free-session/

"How A Spiritual Life Source Coach Can Help You Create the Life You Want"

By Stayce Bowen

My name is Stayce Bowen, and I am a Christian Spiritual Life Source Coach and Healer. I am not a traditional Life Coach. I am a Life Source Coach, a spiritual Healer, healing the lives and souls of other women. As a Life Source Coach, I provide inner divine spiritual direction to help women move towards a life they already possess but may need clarity to tap into.

Our life is a journey, and in order to truly stay the course for the journey we must first understand our origin, our organic self. We cannot understand the life we want unless we first explore where life begins and the plan that was established for our lives. So let's now explore my definition of life, where there is much more to life than just our fleshly human physicality. In my definition of life, our spirit can live without human physical form. However, our physical, fleshly body cannot live without a spirit, so ultimately the spirit gives way to life.

Now let's take a moment to evaluate the definition of the word "source". A definition of "source" is...
1. the beginning or place of origin; and,
2. a book, statement or person supplying information.

When I combined the meanings of the two words, Life and Source, I saw such power, and thus created the title "Life Source Coach".

Now let's explore what Spiritual Life Source Coaching is.

We are all spirit beings having an earthly experience. Life Source Coaching trains you how to connect with your inner spirit.

A Spiritual Life Source coach creates a partnership with you to map out your life plan by returning to your organic self by way of our true beginning in the Garden of Eden where creation of womankind began.

Through "life mapping" we help you create your spiritual profile based on six significant women in the bible and their spiritual characteristics. We design and customize a life mapping plan of practical strengths, weaknesses, goals, childhood and current life structure.

To do this we study the biblical woman and show how, even in her weaknesses, God shows up strong to use her mightily. We study when and how God made the change in her life to provide new direction. We then map out these changes and parallel them to your life.

There is an Eve in every woman, stemming from when we were most complete. But, throughout our patterns of everyday life, many women experience trauma in various forms such as abuse, neglect, molestation, insecurities, abandonment, divorce and many more. Being traumatized causes us to move further away from our spiritual and divine purpose. Spiritual Life Sourcing takes you back to the original Eve within you, to a place of truth, wellness and wholeness.

A Spiritual Life Source Coach ministers to your inner beauty and power. In today's society many of us don't even know who we are, what we truly like, or, furthermore, how we even feel. Through meditations, Vision boards and Heartmath breathing techniques we teach you how to develop that Eve within again. You go from just simply living to truly being alive.

As I stated earlier, we first work with you to build your biblical profile. Then we chart your personality traits (any that you wish to share), and together we categorize you according to one of the six dynamic women of the bible.

After creating your profile, we life-map a road to success for you. We target your main area of interest, such as relationship building, finances, wellness, weight loss, organization structure, parenting, or singleness and dating. Life mapping is strategically planned from where you are currently, to where you want to go. We use spiritual "gardening tools" to excavate, cultivate, and fertilize your spiritual soil, so you reap the most bountiful harvest that God has for you. We take the old ashes and trade them for beauty.

Christian Spiritual life sourcing helps create the life you want by reinforcing your inner "Eve." You were wonderfully created intentionally by God, the same God who in his majestic omnipotence made all of creation and then sat back and said "It is good." The word of God is our basic instruction for life, and his instructions were designed to speak to your spirit.

The Bible is often called the "Good News", and thus our life is good news! By disarming a worldly belief system and reconnecting with your spiritual purpose, you can begin to live the life that you may only pretend you are having.

Life Source coaching equips you with the supernatural tools and resources to be more than a champion. For example, one of the resources that I've developed for Life Sourcing is called, "Surgery for the Soul." This powerful tool says it all in its name!

Although it specifically targets our soul and spirit, Surgery for the Soul is designed and crafted much like actual surgery. There is a prognosis, a surgeon, operating tools, and a sterile environment. Often the spirit of a woman is wounded and needs "surgery." Surgery for the Soul is the prescription for her spiritual healing.

After your diagnosis, we begin your rehabilitation plan, mapping out your spiritual medicine, and then you're off to recovery. The benefits to Surgery for the Soul are many. Women in recovery have gone on to be successful in areas of life such as marriages, business affairs, financial prosperity, and a host of other endeavors.

Spiritual sickness is something that requires a spiritual surgeon. (Not many doctors are dedicated to the true internal terminal illness of your soul.) There is nothing more drastic or deadly than an unhealed spirit, because it is our spiritual awareness and spiritual conscience that make up who we are. Women today are being measured from the outside, but we cannot be built from the outside. Women are built from the inside out.

Outward appearances such as sex appeal, which sells, are not the only qualities of a beautiful and powerful woman. Did you know that it is your spiritual countenance that makes you beautiful? The ability to walk in your own truth is what gives you beauty and power. Spiritual coaching and Surgery for the Soul breaks worldly chains that shackle us to misconceptions about who we are.

Spiritual Life Coaching and Life Mapping can create the life you ultimately have been dreaming of. You are created in the image of excellence. So rejoice. You are a masterpiece handcrafted with the breath of life by the Master himself. You are not an accident. You are a unique vessel called to fulfill a mission on earth. You have been promised to live and live more abundantly.

You were given birthright promises as an heir to the Kingdom.

Besides being a Spiritual Life Source Coach, I am also the Glam Majesty of a spiritual women's empowerment Sisterhood recognized as, "Glam Moms." I called myself the "Glam Majesty" because it was more fun and "diva-ish", as opposed to Founder, President and all of those other boring titles.

My organization, Glam Moms, can be found on the web at www.glammoms.org (We are under a new and improved launch coming soon.) Glam Moms is designed specifically for the wounded soul of a woman. We provide the prescription for her healing by intertwining the freedom of her spirit with that of being a "Gardener" and tending to her "garden." We are here to embrace your needs while maintaining your femininity.

Many Glam Moms are entrepreneurs. We are strong. We work in and out of the home. We are glamorous and always grateful for what God has done and is doing. Our focus is on inner beauty and power.

Glam Moms is a resource to spiritually uplift and redirect women. We are a collaborative of new millennial women claiming the Proverbs 31 woman birthright *"Our focus is one...who can find a virtuous woman for her price is far above rubies."* We are not just a social organization---we are an extraordinary Coaching platform.

About the Author

Stayce Wilson-Bowen
Spiritual Life Source Coach

Glam Moms (Surgery for the Soul)
Glammoms.org

Stayce Wilson-Bowen-Glam Moms and Surgery for the Soul
Life Source Guide
Philadelphia, PA.

Beautiful and powerful from the inside out, Stayce serves as an Agent of Change, a Life Source guide and Healer. Stayce's approach to coaching is to be a life source guide directing women back to their divine origin, the Garden of Eden where God created and finished everything...and saw that it was good. Creating a safe place for women to "go back to their soil, toil their garden, cultivate and excavate" through their pain and embrace abundance in every area of their life.

"The Power Of Life Coaching To Help You Create The Life You Want: Enhancing Your Quality Of Life And Well-Being"

By Luz Jaramillo

How my life challenges and achievements helped me become a happy and successful life coach and create the life I want.

As a child, I struggled with learning difficulties, memory problems, an eating disorder, and chronic stress. I lacked confidence and possessed low self-esteem. School work was very challenging and learning any new task was difficult. I was never able to focus while reading, and it was tough for me to complete reading one full book. My internal dialogue told me: *I am not good enough, I am not smart enough, I cannot do it.* This led me to find comfort in eating. Whenever I felt stress, I would to get up and grab some food.

As an adult, I was a constant worrier, negative about my future, and prone to self-pity. I had been listening to my internal voice for years telling me I could not stop eating and I could not succeed in my personal or professional life. I felt stuck in many situations in my life. I had little control over my thoughts and often I just let my brain tell me what I wanted to hear.

I knew I had a purpose and needed to do something to change myself, but I was so focused on my problems that I didn't know where to start. How could I, someone with so many personal challenges, learn to be independent and successful and become who I wanted to be? I never imagined I would one day be able to create my own business, write a book, or even be successful at what I do.

Despite all my challenges with learning new information and recalling facts, through hard work and determination I was able to complete my Social Work degree. I worked for almost 20 years with the geriatric population at assisted living institutions. I loved that job. It was so fulfilling to work with people and to be able to help them in many ways. Most of my clients had Alzheimer's or dementia. I felt a strong connection with them since I could relate because of my own memory problems.

What impacted me the most throughout my job experience was that these seniors had been very successful in their lives. They were all financially well off, living in very comfortable, luxurious facilities with the support of loving families, but most of them, were unhappy. It always came to my mind that they had worked so hard all their lives only to end up with a poor level of well-being all because of the low cognitive functioning. That made me realized how important it is to maintain a healthy brain.

At that time, I had small children and I resigned from my job to dedicate my time to raise them. I knew I was fortunate to be able to make this choice, and I thought it would lead to more happiness and fulfillment, but all the time at home, without the structure of work, caused my eating and stress issues to spiral out of control. Why was I still unhappy when I thought that I was supposed to be living my dream?

To fight off the despair, I decided to learn about new ways of self-help and healing. I researched and studied areas of personal development such as, the science of well-being, the law of attraction, spirituality, and neuroscience. One of the topics that fascinated me the most was what makes a person successful and the key for them to be extraordinary. I didn't want to focus only on areas of financial success, I also wanted to learn how to change my mindset to be as happy and healthy as possible.

When I started to research the new material, my learning difficulties and negative self-talk came to the surface again. I didn't know how I was going to learn all of this, I just knew I had to do something. I was afraid and stressed all the time, but my desire was stronger than my fear. I used my struggles to help me learn from my old experiences and develop new skills that enabled me to be stronger. I knew I needed to create ways to improve my focus, productivity, and memory, so I started to investigate how the brain works and how to improve my capacities even with my limitations. I became obsessive and fascinated not only for my own sake but also to help others.

I began my journey to create my new life. I became certified in Neuro-linguistic Programming (NLP), which studies the connection between language and thoughts and teaches you ways to reprogram your brain. It helps you think and talk positively to reach the goals you want to improve your life.

I completed my certifications as a Life Coach, a Master NLP, and a Brain Health Coach with great success. I used scientific methods to engage my brain consciously and unconsciously to get tangible results. I was able to heal my learning disabilities and eating disorders and develop a sense of confidence that I never known before. My concentration, memory, and ability to focus were so radically improved that all I wanted to do was read books to increase my knowledge. I went on to complete courses in neuroplasticity (the brain's ability to create new synapses and changes in structure and chemistry), stress management, eating disorder awareness, and mindfulness.

I wanted to fully understand and claim the blessings that were available to me and to help other people do the same. As I mastered the art and science of how to manifest success in every area of my life, I learned how to apply it consistently and effectively, not only in my own life, but in the lives of the people I met.

Since I began this journey five years ago, I have accomplished 125 of the 130 goals that I set for myself. I now have the life I dreamed of. All of my life changes have motivated me to focus on being successful at what I do. I now find easy ways to cope with stress. I love and accept my body, and no longer struggle with low self-esteem. Today, I nourish my body and soul with a lifestyle that brings me health, happiness, fulfillment, and peace. I have plenty of free time to spend with my loving husband and two amazing children, to travel, and to enjoy the present. This life can be possible for you as well. My state of well-being is amazing. I wake up every morning happy and energized because I know that I get to spend the day doing what I love as a life coach. And every day I get to create my own dream life!

My point is not to brag about me; it is to tell you that all of this is possible for you. The most important thing for me is that I know I am meant to help others build a life they love living. I've devoted my life to helping as many people as possible so that no one goes without living the life they were created to live. I have used my studies and research, to create one of the best brain-based approaches to help you achieve the quality of life and well-being you deserve. Now my goal is to help you find the best possible ways to enhance your capacities and success, reach any goal, and build the life of your dreams. Many people have approached me, asking how they can do what I'm doing, and this is my gift to you.

The most important thing is to have the certainty that you will be able to do this too. That is one of the keys to success: to be 100 percent sure that it is going to happen, that any goal you set in your mind you believe you have already achieved.

Some of us have so many subconscious, negative beliefs that we are not even aware they exist. Beliefs such as *I am not good enough, I cannot stop eating, I don't have talent, I don't have the skills, I cannot write, I make a lot of mistakes.* These beliefs start from childhood before you are even seven years old. It's essential to discover and eliminate them to start owning a new and more empowering belief system.

This strategy works when applied to any aspect of your life. When you are out of your comfort zone, it can be stressful, but if you focus on the on your vision you can achieve what you want. It is all about uncovering and eliminating negative beliefs that have unknowingly controlled our lives since childhood. Your beliefs can keep you stuck or make you better. If you are sure you cannot do it, your unconscious mind believes that. When you learn to be aware of your negative beliefs, you will be able to switch your thoughts. I will teach you that with my program.

Our negative beliefs are blocking us from all of the possibilities life holds for us. Saying prayers and repeating positive affirmations do not always work, but if you have the certainty and the faith that things are going to change, anything is possible. The transformational tools that I use in my program are based in the science of how our minds, body, energy, emotions, spirituality, and thoughts work together — and most importantly in the science of how the brain works.

I changed my life through science and NLP. That's why my mission is to work with people who desire a state of freedom. Find a decision you really want to make; don't worry about "the how", focus on "the why". I learned to teach the brain to focus on the outcome instead of thinking the negative beliefs and false statements. I wasn't sure of how to do it, but I had the certainty that it was going to be done.

I will teach you how to replace negative beliefs with tools that will increase your capabilities and remove your limitations. When you change your negative beliefs, a fantastic change in your life happens. You will learn to switch words and thoughts for a positive reaction. Through visualization, you will learn to use all of your senses to visualize your goals as if you have already achieved them.

How my program can help you create the life you want

"Whatever your mind can conceive and believe, it can achieve." ~Napoleon Hill

The brain is the most important organ of the body, and we have programmed it with either wrong or right information since our childhood. We cannot change the past, but we can change the present and future by understanding how the brain works and how to use it for the best benefit possible. The power is within you!

I have created a program with techniques and strategies that are research-based and easy to understand, to help you reach your goals. I do one-on-one coaching to connect with clients either in person, on the phone, or over the Internet. My usual session is 60 minutes each week. I also offer group coaching, which is like one-on-one coaching but allows me to serve more people in the same amount of time. I host live events, where I enjoy interacting with clients in person and helping a lot of people get a fast start and learn a great deal in a short period.

My program is grounded in evidence-based research and the latest neuroscientific discoveries to accelerate the process of building your brain neurons for better capacity and productivity. Not only will you enhance your brain capacity, but you will also strengthen your mindset to eliminate the limited beliefs that are barriers to achieving your goals. You will master your confidence and control your behaviors, increase your focus and concentration, find better ways to cope with stress in any circumstance—and most importantly—achieve success in any area.

I will provide essential information about how the brain works and how to maintain a healthy brain, as well as techniques to eliminate automatic negative thoughts, overthinking, and social comparison. We will also focus on practicing kindness, making social connections, and developing strategies for coping with stress. And you will learn ways to forgive, since scientific studies show that forgiving others helps enhance your own well-being.

I want to be clear that every technique is as effective as the studies report but all significant life changes require considerable effort. There is no result without action. Happiness, success, and well-being are indeed within your reach. What works for you may not work for someone else. The reason you haven't yet been able to accomplish your goals is that you need to find the specific techniques that work best for you so you can persist. Like many diets and self-help programs, there is no magic strategy that will help every person. That is why with my program, I provide support and accountability to find the best happiness-enhancing, health-boosting strategies that work best for your values, motivations, goals, and resources.

I will work with your strengths and talents to discover what motivates you. Some of my clients prefer to pursue significant life goals such as getting the job of their dreams, while others are looking for more general ways to boost happiness. For that reason, I focus on different techniques based on your particular dreams and desires.

With each of my clients, I evaluate different strategies that work best for an individual personalized approach. When we create your individualized plan, tailored to your specific needs and goals, you will feel more engaged and motivated to commit yourself to change. I have open communication with my clients about how they think about their progress. A goal can be achieved in several ways if you know the right strategy and the mindset for success. One of the reasons people fail in their efforts is because, unfortunately, they choose the wrong plan or approach. Because of that, they lack persistence and are unable to follow through. I find the right plan for my clients and provide the support and guidance so they can fully commit.

I have developed a comprehensive initial assessment to incorporate all the different ways of measuring what fits your needs, and lifestyle so, we can determinate what techniques are more valuable for you to try. Completing my assessment enables me to help you, but it also lets you define what you want for yourself. If you assess with motivation, you will continue to put effort into the desire and will be more likely to succeed. If you don't give enough value to the initial assessment, however, then we may choose the wrong technique, which may lead to decreased motivation. You need to be persistent at it. If one technique fits you at first but then it does not motivate you, we evaluate the results and reasons. Based on my personal experience and my client's accomplishments, I have concluded that it is important to make multiple attempts to succeed. You may find one or many techniques that fit you well, based on the strategies suggested.

Evaluating your lifestyle is an essential part of the success of the program. We will work together to develop a program designed to suit your personal needs. If you have a stressful life and lack time, then I will recommend methods that will only take you two minutes a day and provide other techniques that you can do quickly and that will benefit you the most.

Your belief system is also very important. Some of my clients are very religious, some are spiritual, while others have a more secular approach to life. That is why it is so important for me to understand your background so I can select techniques that are specially designed to fit your needs.

My areas of expertise focus on clients who struggle with emotional eating or binge eating and helping them to create healthy, sustainable lifestyle habits. Another area of concentration is improving mental focus, attention and productivity. I have some clients who want to optimize brain health and prevent cognitive impairment. Others are entrepreneurs who come to me to find ways to cope with the demands of their high-stress lifestyles. The secret is to establish which strategies suit you best. Once we determine that, then half of the battle is won. The way to achieve your results is in your hands.

Some of my clients have achieved such great success on their journey that they want to help other people by coaching as well. I want you to think about something fundamental. If you enjoy teaching people, if it is important to you to help other people succeed and reach their dreams, if you believe in people's ability to create the lives they desire, if you want to learn more about the principles of success, if you refuse to give up quickly, and/or if you want to be your own boss, you have the potential to be a fantastic life coach.

Life coaching can be one of the most rewarding, impactful, lifestyle-friendly, and lucrative careers in the world. If you are looking to become a life coach like me, I will mentor you to identify the dreams and desires that make you feel authentically happy and fulfilled.

The best type of mentor is one who's using a business model you want to mimic, and who's willing to teach you, step by step, the process of building and running it successfully. I want to work with you.

I will help you remove the negative mindsets, habits, and other obstacles that are holding you back. I will help you create a plan to turn your dreams into reality. I provide one-on-one coaching to create a productive action plan for finding joy in helping people. You need a mentor who can help you avoid the difficulties they've faced so that you can model the success they've created.

Work with me to learn step-by-step techniques in Neuro-linguistic Programming, neuroplasticity, mindfulness or savoring life joys, mindset, gratitude, spirituality or religion, and meditation, as well as brain-training exercises, and the best ways to take care of your body. We will explore with positive affirmations, cultivating optimism, and visualization exercises to make positive switches in your unconscious mind to replace your limited beliefs and habits with extraordinary ones.

About the Author

Luz Jaramillo, Brainbodycoach

I grew up in Columbia and came to the United States as an adult because it had always been a dream of mine. I graduated as a Master Social Worker with more than 20 years of experience. I am also a Certified Dementia Practitioner (CDP) from the National Council of Certified Dementia. I became certified in Neuro-linguistic Programming (NLP) at INLP Center and International NLP Association, which studies the connection between language and thoughts, and teaches you ways to reprogram your brain. It helps you think and talk positively to reach goals you have to improve your life.

I completed my certifications as a Life Coach, a Master NLP, and a Brain Health Coach at Amen University. I went on to complete courses in Neuroplasticity, Metabolic Health & Fitness Coach Certificate, Stress Coach Certificate: Stress Management Life Coaching, Eating Disorder Awareness Diploma from The International Alliance of Holistic Therapist, and Master practitioner in Mindfulness. I am a member of the International Association of Professional Life Coach (IAPLC). I saw so much change in myself that I am now committed to bringing this work to others.

I created my own company, Brainbodycoach, Inc. and now I help individuals who are dealing with emotional or binge eating, high levels of stress, brain fog, low focus and productivity, mental decline, or those who just want to improve their quality of life. I provide a holistic coaching process that uses cognitive, science-based techniques that promote a healthy lifestyle, so you can lead a happy, healthy, fulfilling and prosperous life.

Go to: https://brainbodycoach.com to select a time for a 30-minute non-obligation session and Request your free copy of videos *"The 5 Mindset Shifts To Enhance Your Life!"*

I look forward to hearing from you:
Contact: luz@brainbodycoach.com
https://brainbodycoach.com/
https://www.instagram.com/brainbodycoach
https://www.facebook.com/brainbodycoach

"What Do You Really, Really Want?"

By Susie Briscoe

How Do You Decide on the Life You Want?

Looking at this from all directions, but mainly from a business angle, I've decided to take inspiration from an unusual source for this chapter, and quote the Spice Girls from their 1990's massive world number one hit: "Tell Me What You Want, What You Really, *Really* Want? Then I'll Tell You What I Want, What I Really, *Really* Want!" Who knew that a group of young English girls in a girl band, virtually straight out of school, would come up with such a good coaching question!

We all think we know the answer to this... we simply want to create the best life for ourselves! But what does that really mean? It means the best of everything we want, desire, need, or crave... doesn't it? It depends on whether we wish to pursue an academic pathway leading to degrees and/or specialty careers, for example a World-Renowned Heart Surgeon such as Devi Prasad Shetty or Hasnat Khan: they would certainly need to achieve credibility by attaining various levels of academic knowledge and then further specialty knowledge in the field of medicine.

However if you wish to have a more sporty approach to creating your best life by surfing in the summer and skiing in the winter then your requirement would be to get extremely fit and learn how to surf (perhaps also include water-skiing) and snow-ski, even if you weren't going to do it at a professional level.

This means we need to look at the life we are living. Here I am reminded of the tourist who is a business man – very high powered, earning a lot of money and at the top of his game, with a beautiful wife and family – he hardly ever sees them, but he knows they are there, because doesn't he always make sure that they are happy and have everything they want? Yes of course he does – that's his duty and mission in life – and he takes his beautiful wife and children on the most fantastic holidays to the most glamorous, remote and very beautiful places – this year it's to islands in the tropics.

On the first day of their holiday the man – let's call him Gary – asks the very exclusive boutique hotel concierge to get him a boat as he wants to take his family out for an entire day marlin fishing and cruising up and down the coast.

He wanders down to the marina and finds the boat they will be hiring for the day, and the owner of the boat, let's call him Enrique, greets him with a warm handshake and smile. They set out and have a fabulous day. Gary enjoys talking to Enrique and they have many discussions on life and the meaning thereof, amongst other far-ranging topics.

Gary hires Enrique and his small boat every day of his holiday and recognizes how relaxed and happy this simple fisherman is. It makes him want to help him, and because Gary is so successful, he suggests that they might go into business together, or even that he just backs him in a business endeavor. Gary is seeing opportunities that he feels Enrique has not thought of and wants to mentor him to become a big-shot fisherman and tourist guide; he proposes that Enrique could have several ships in a marina in one of the larger coastal cities– start with just one or two and then build up a whole fleet.

Enrique is very surprised and asks what that would achieve. Gary replies that he would be able to have an amazing life similar to his own – a lovely house, great opportunities for his family to meet different people to those in their small community. Enrique poses the question again and Gary triumphantly says so that he could finally retire and have the life of his dreams with a boat down here with no worries.

Imagine Gary's surprise when Enrique says: "I have that already. Each day I can take my boat out; my family are well cared for and have everything they need, and they get to meet really interesting people such as yourself (Gary) and your family". Gary is perplexed. It hadn't occurred to him that not everyone wants to be a big shot in business. It didn't mean that either man had not achieved well in his own field; they had just done it differently.

Gary had gone the academic route: school, college/university and then specialist business school. Enrique had learnt everything that his father and grandfather could teach him; his education and that of his children was ongoing by virtue of what they learnt from tourists that came into their lives. They had both had to learn and work hard to achieve their results and each had gained credibility from the way they had learnt, grown and continued to grow and learn from and about life. Their values were good and relevant – just different. Each had succeeded in creating a life that they really wanted it was just their routes were diverse.

This is apt at so many levels. I cannot remember the first time I heard this story, but it resonated with me as well as made a lot of sense. We, in the so-called western world, believe we have all the solutions to every question or dilemma, but what if we are asking the wrong questions of ourselves. This takes me back to what it is that we really want from our life. Have we actually stopped to ask this question? Or other similar questions, which would make us take stock of where we are on our own journey and what our purpose and mission is? What is it that is important to us and what are our values? What are the ethical and moral codes by which we navigate our way through life? How possible is it to incorporate these into our business life?

That's quite a long lead in to the point I want to consider during this chapter. Not everybody wants the same thing, so what is it that you want? Before you are able to create your best life ever, you have to understand what that is - and what it isn't. How does it all look, feel, smell, and taste. When you listen what do you hear?

Let's say you adore cats, but especially one breed – the Burmese – and you want to be known as **the** number one authority and go-to person across the whole world. If you are writing a blog about Burmese cats, nobody really cares if you have a doctorate. However, they **do** care whether or not you know anything about Burmese cats –- and it helps if you actually have one yourself (or have previously owned at least one). But just tell them that Burmese cats have short, bushy tails and are ginger and white - and all credibility is gone with your audience immediately.

You see, being the world's go-to number one authority requires you to have put in the hard yards and actually know what you are writing about, so that your public knows that **you** know what you're talking about. That's what we call credibility. When you get right down to it, credibility means that you are believable - and you deliver the goods that prove this. It's about knowing how to communicate and connect most effectively and directly so that your ideal clients or customers unhesitatingly know *you* are the best person to help them in your niche, whatever that niche is.

Just for the record, I do adore cats, and my own personal favorite is not necessarily a real breed but maybe a bit of a mixture: any rescue cat that is black, extremely small (possibly the runt of the litter) and has an oriental look to its face... for that cat I will walk across hot coals and provide it with a perfect and comfortable home, whatever its needs. Doing this makes me happy, brings me joy, and relaxes me just to know that this tiny black moggy (a colloquial and affectionate word for cat) is in my world in some way. So that small addition to my family helps to create a tiny part of my perfect life.

What else would you add to your perfect life? – possibly not cats. In all probability your own needs and desires may be very different to mine. Let's take a look at some things that might contribute to helping you work out what your perfect life is in particular looking towards your business life.

Step One: Put the Past into Perspective - and Words

It's about credibility and how you see yourself. Whatever path you decide to take in life, you first of all need to know that you are good at it and that others recognize your expertise. We often say belief and self-esteem come from within, but what about looking at choices in your business life? To live the life you want may depend on you being considered, at the very least, good at what you do in order for you to be able to command the respect and/or money required to live this life.

People will tell you that it takes years to build up credibility - and to a point, that's true: But think back to experts who you gave your trust to. Was there anyone who gained your trust and interest instantly? Did you find yourself either wishing you were exactly like that professional - or that you could be coached by her? If so, take out a notepad and detail exactly what happened - and why you felt the way you did.

Exercise 1.

- **What caught your attention?** (Was it an example? A statement? Someone talking about exactly what you needed right that moment?)
- **What did you feel?** (Be as detailed as possible, no matter how self-conscious or silly that makes you feel.)
- **What did that person offer?** (And how much it resonated with you.)
- **What did you buy?** (And why you bought it.)
- **How well did your purchase deliver?** (Was it the solution that was promised? Did you get at least one valuable, tangible "gem" from it that made your life better in some way?)
- **How hard did you have to work to continue the relationship?** (Did you remember who that person was, the next time they emailed? Did their follow-up email come after an interval that felt natural? Were you eager for more?)

What most likely stands out in your mind, if you remember an expert like this, might well be that the connection was instant.

Don't just remember your introduction to this expert - make actual notes about it. And now the most important question - the one the directly relates to your field of expertise:

- *Why was the connection instant?*

Step Two: Determine What Credentials/Authorizations You Need to Succeed

I'm still sticking with credentials and how you see yourself to help you discover what you need for your best life. Your answer to "Why was the connection instant?" immediately determines what you need in order to attain credibility for your best life. If you answered that the connection was instant because that particular research chemist is doing the job you want to do, you definitely **do** need credentials such as doctorates and degrees.

If you answered about the Burmese cat owner, "her problem with Tipsy exactly described the weird situation I'm going through with Rollo right now" then you aren't interested in her credentials: You want to know her solution - and you're reassured that she experienced it with her own Burmese cat.

If you are trying to enter a field where certain professional organizations hold sway, you need to show your clientele that you are a member in good standing - and the more acknowledgment you have from that organization in the way of awards and accreditation, the more reassured your specific target market will feel.

So, take your notepad and write down what type of "credentials" you need for your particular field:

Exercise 2:

- Degrees
- Certificates
- Accreditation
- Personal experience
- Practical, working experience

If you are having trouble narrowing this down, proceed to the next step…

Step Three: Certification and Credentials - Are they Necessary to Live the Life You Want?

Do any of your most successful competitors have degrees or accreditation? If so, do they display their degrees after their names? Do they show accreditation stamps or professional organization logos prominently on their blogs or websites?

If they do, then it's a sure bet accreditation is important, even if only legally. Consider taking courses or joining the same professional organizations, if you need to do so - or else figure out another way you are going to show professional credibility. (For example, in Canada, interior designers and draftspersons legally need to acquire a B.C.I.N. number[1] before they can practice.)

You can still practice as an architectural technologist if you don't have one - but you need to be ready to associate with or hire a fellow professional who does possess a B.C.I.N. and who is ready to provide that number on stamped drawings.

One way to display your credentials would be to highlight your awards, if your design experience went back a long way, and/or briefly talk about your major industry-breakthrough achievements. (e.g. "Invented the circular, self-closing skylight for Cargill and Company, 1989")

And, of course, display your results - before and after shots of a client's renovation project, for example. (Happy or proud

---

[1] Building Code Identification Number

clients are usually pleased to give permission and provide photographs - and testimonials. But you have to ask them - and the best time to do that is in your second consultation, so that you are setting them up for your specific request when the job is done - *not afterwards*.)

If you were an interior designer, you would also see, while checking out B.C.I.N. certification, that requirements changed in 2017: A three-year college diploma will no longer be adequate for certification. You would need "a CIDA-accredited bachelor's degree program as the minimum education requirement".

Fortunately, most online marketers don't need such stringent and specific certification - and degrees are not always a guarantee of stronger credibility if they are too general or not relevant to your client's need today: However, one factor you do need to check carefully is whether or not certain certifications are required <u>by law</u>.

To relate this with online marketing examples:
- You do, by law, need a disclaimer page about affiliate earnings, if you have affiliate links on any of your pages.
- Certain types of coaches don't need anything more than visible, proven experience. Others, however, by law need highly specific professional accreditations to practice.

You can also display seals and insignia from your professional organizations to bolster your professional image - and the beauty of these organizations is their courses are not necessarily three-year courses. For example, a licensed plumber could increase the credibility of his site with any number of professional logos after his contact information - the customer doesn't need to know that the snazzy "CPDA" logo really means he took a week-long course in effluent pumps with the Cochrane Professional Dealers Association.

To summarize: certification, degrees and credentials are sometimes required by law in certain fields, but displaying or talking about other credentials and certification is only as strong as the way you position and present them. If you are able to show a potential client *your* membership in a certain body is to *her* advantage, go for it!

And everybody, in any field, had better keep their ears to the ground to find out what new laws are going to be put into effect and which credentials are soon going to be required.

But when deciding which of your accreditations to highlight or display, the main point to keep in mind is:

- Show what is legally required for your industry and field
- Show what your customer or client most urgently needs/wants to see

If you don't need to clutter up a website talking for two pages about your credentials or degrees, don't.   Focus on proven results.

Step Four: Mining your Competition

We spoke earlier about checking out your main competition to see how they positioned their own credibility. This step is always relevant.

Exercise 3:
You need to ask yourself:
- "What sells my competitor to her clients?"

- "What does she present that I don't have?"
- "What advantages do I have that she doesn't?"
- "What are her clients saying? What are they praising/complaining about?"

These are big clues to help you start planning how you are going to boost your own online credibility.

Step Five: Storytelling

The best way to create credibility lies in two simple actions:
- Think of your website as your "story"
- Live your story in social networks, media, YouTube videos, articles, guest spots and live venues

But there's one key point here: Your story has to mirror your ideal customer or clients. Show her you totally understand her challenges and can provide what she has trouble discovering.

In other words, both customers and clients have to be able to and feel comfortable with you.

If you go back to our first exercise, where you thought of a professional that you connected with instantly after reading an article or a post on their website, your connection to their story is most likely the reason - you found yourself saying: "It's as if she was talking about me!" Or: "Yes! That's EXACTLY what I've been trying to tell people I'm having trouble with!"

The best way to give your story credibility is to be real: Just tell it like it is.

Then edit out anything that doesn't relate to your customers.

For example, they don't need to know about your epiphany with bird-watching if your website is there to help them get into the best physical shape of your life - unless you tell your bird-watching story to demonstrate that unwittingly, as you were hiking miles of trails in search of the rare stomach-catcher warbler, you were toning your leg muscles and losing weight without thinking about it (relevance).

Here's how to tell a great story - one that will resonate with your customer or client:

1. **Find out their biggest concern, problem, desire or need**
   Dig deep. Think about what you're reading, hearing and what they are showing you.
   - For example, when a client says, "I need someone to do my bookkeeping", yes, he may mean it literally - but stop. What they could really be saying is any of the following:
   - "I hate bookkeeping. Mathematics makes me break out in hives."
   - "I can do it, but I don't make money when I do my own books - I make it when I design a website."
   - "I feel frazzled and overwhelmed with my business."
   - "I need to keep in a creative-flow state of mind, and bookkeeping knocks me out of that."

The really brilliant storytellers don't speak just to their clients' visible problems: It's when they tap into the hidden fear, desire or frustration underneath the surface - and address that hidden issue directly - that they create credibility.

2. **Be yourself.**
   Speak to your clients with your own voice. People who think they need to put on an "image" do exactly that - and people see through insincerity quicker online today than in the Internet's infancy.

When people read your articles or website posts, they must hear the same voice you use when you speak to them. In their minds, there should be no difference between reading what you've written and listening to your podcast.

Reveal just enough of yourself to connect emotionally - to use yourself as an example. Focus on your client or customer.

3. Be repetitive.

Not like a broken record but communicate in the way your audience has come to expect. Use templates to help create that repetitive consistency. Create regular, recurring features people can look forward to and remember.

There's a reason that little children love stories based on simple repetition. Repetition means structure; and structure equals "safety"; Safety equals credibility.

Even when you present wildly different theories or products, presenting them stamped with elements of repetition - your company colors, your logo, your price structure - helps to reassure those ready to take your exciting new/next step.

4. Be real.

We've talked about repetition and consistency and safety for your audience. When it comes to you, however, be prepared to take risks. Reveal yourself if you want your customer to view you as a real person who actually does understand her life circumstances. If you sit comfortably, several stories-high above your customer, seemingly being perfect all your life, they will *never* relate to you (no matter how much they might envy you).

If they know you've had the same weaknesses, struggles, challenges and failures, it will mean much more to your customers when they see you now, having surpassed these. This is the **hero's journey** – proof they can really do what you do and get to where you're sitting.

That's called "credibility" too - and it's the most important sort: it's emotional credibility.

It's all about relevance; it's not really about you. It's only ever about your customer or client, and her particular journey.

Step Six: Your Audience

To prove credibility, you have to totally understand your particular, unique audience - and those who search and live online generally.

Consumers have gotten better at spotting phonies, which means they require more solid proof of your abilities.

On the other hand, barriers to online purchasing have dropped. While online security continues to be an issue of concern, there is no longer a huge fear preventing the majority of shoppers - particularly those with cell phones - from parting with credit card information on line.

You will always get the odd client who insists on looking over your shoulder or micro-controlling every step of a project; then complains about cost overages, which have resulted from this micro managing.

These are the human character traits and cultural trends you have to consider, anticipate and plan for, when setting up your services and website. The more thoroughly you can anticipate, the better you can prevent misunderstandings or dissatisfaction – remember: happy clients and customers mean better testimonials and better recommendations.

Better recommendations mean greater credibility.

Step Seven: Practical Experience

You don't always need to have literally "walked the walk" - but if you haven't done so, you do need to make sure that you:

- Thoroughly understand what you are sharing, selling or teaching - and that what you share is valid and valuable.
- Provide well-researched, accurate facts, products and information your ideal paying client or customer can successfully use.

The best way to be credible is to genuinely focus on serving your client or customer. Care about their problems. Find real solutions. And when you've found that solution, go back and re-think it again: Is there any way you can go a step further by:

- Making it better
- Making it simpler

When you value yourself and value your customer, it is much easier to provide the perfect solution for everyone.

- The more practical experience you have in your chosen field, the more confident you'll feel. The more confident you feel, the more confidence you will project.
- The more practical experience you have in your chosen field, the less you will have to talk about yourself; the more others will positively talk about and recommend you.

But it would be naive to think you can sit back and all this wonderful buzz and credibility will happen. You need to promote yourself in the right places; how much promotion depends on how well known you already are on the web, how much of a celebrity or expert you are known as in your field and how wide your reach is.

For example, if you were a household name in the dog world, like Cesar Milan, not only would you have a highly professional, well-paid team to manage promotion and advertising, but also you would be seen in every household across North America in your TV shows.

People would be able to see from your TV shows that your dog training gets results and provides exceptional solutions.

You may not have a big budget or even a team (yet), but you can duplicate these strategies - and results - quite easily, using the following three suggestions:

1. Show - don't tell
Is yours a tactile or physical skill? Create a video series and start sharing it.

Focus on the narrowest area of skill you most want to be known for - preferably something your competitors have not yet managed to successfully cover - and build your series around that.

For example, if you are a master weaver and your big product is a brand-new type of loom targeted at serious craft weavers building up experience, create a video series on different types of looms. Each episode in your series should demonstrate a different loom type: i.e.
- Episode One: Weaving on a Rigid Heddle Loom
- Episode Two: Weaving on a Back-Strap Loom

- Episode Three: Weaving on a Tapestry Frame Loom

And so forth.

Finally, release a video demonstrating your brand new, original loom:

- Episode Six: The Murray Lightweight Portable Jack Loom

(That's yours!)

It's up to you to decide on the intervals between episode releases but use the time between episodes to get the word out about your series and ask other weavers to share your links.

Do your best to make sure each episode:

- Identifies the most common glitch or problem people experience with whatever you're demonstrating
- Shows them a ridiculously easy or logical way to solve this

Don't overwhelm them with industry jargon or try to show off your knowledge - focus your attention one-hundred-and-ten percent on helping them overcome and master their one big problem with whatever component you're showing them.

Write posts about your videos, treating your written post content as a "teaser" and making sure your video is embedded in the post, so people don't feel like they have to leave your site to view the video.

Take it one step further, and include actual screen shots from your video in your post, so that people can see instantly - at a glance - what they're going to learn.

Notice that videos perform one other valuable service in helping you establish visibility (the first step to credibility): People see your face in what feels like "real time". They see your facial expressions they hear your tone of voice; they experience your confidence and mastery of your topic.

A video series is the next best thing to presenting courses and workshops in person - and it's always available on YouTube, every time someone types in this instance, "jack looms".

Always make sure your social posts, podcasts, webinars and videos include calls to action, of course, but these should flow naturally from each piece of content - your calls to action must never feel like a sales blitz.

2. Stay Updated in your Field
If you want to be regarded as the go-to person and ultimate authority in your topic or field, make a commitment to staying on top of new developments and keep up with your Continual Professional Development (CPD).

Step Eight: Authenticity

If you want to build credibility, people have to feel that they can trust you absolutely. Speaking to them with your whole focus on them and their needs is only the first step in making sure this trust develops.

Here's how you can develop it further:

1. **Be Transparent**

   If you don't know the answer to something, say so, simply and plainly. Then either promise to find out, giving a date you'll do this by, or refer them to another industry peer who can help them.

2. **Build your Reputation**

   People also need to know:
   - What you stand for
   - What they can count on you to provide
   - What you can help them with
   - What you won't do

   This means you need to know these things too - and live by them.

3. **Learn to Listen**

   What makes someone trust another person? Many things: But high on the list is "feeling that the expert you're talking to cares".

   Surprisingly, too many experts undermine themselves in this area by not actively listening. Instead, they're too busy thinking of the perfect thing to say (and anticipating what the person they are talking to is trying to share). The result? The person talking to them feels cut off when the "expert" begins to talk over the top of them, anxious to dispense his knowledge.

   That person may feel unheard, belittled, boring or any other variety of negative emotions.

   Really listen. Remember, you may have heard the identical question or problem five hundred times before, but it's new to your questioner.

Real listening involves:

- Acknowledging
- Mirroring back
- Re-stating the person's main point, if necessary, to ensure you've got it right
- Waiting till your questioner has finished speaking before offering your ideas

Know your mission. Know your values. And don't be afraid to say, "I don't know - but I can find out..."

Step Nine: Reassurance

While you're busy being authentic, do make sure you use professional-quality profile photos on all your sites and social platforms (preferably versions of the same photo). Make sure your photo is current and updated regularly. There's nothing like letting your audience meet you in person and then discover someone 90lbs. heavier and twenty-two years older than that perfect profile photo; this is guaranteed to bewilder and disappoint them.

Using honest, current profile photos is enhanced by using videos, so that people can see how you operate in "real time".

There are other ways to provide reassurance – which is a big part of credibility building - to your target audience.

Here are three of the easiest and most important ways to provide reassurance:

1. **Delivery**

   To build credibility, deliver exactly what you promised and make sure it easily does exactly what you said it would.

   Don't include nasty little surprises such as "you can only solve your big problem if you upgrade to my Big-Ticket Product". If you promised your Little Ticket Product would do A, B and C, then under no circumstances just give your customer A and B - and then force them to upgrade, to receive C!

   If you provide upsells, make sure they are presented as options for people who want more.

   And it's always a good thing if you provide more than they asked for, but it's not strictly necessary as long as "what you promised" more than delights.

   A customer/client may become overwhelmed if you bombard them with dozens or hundreds of other "bonuses" - particularly when these:
   - Are not directly related to the product your customer bought
   - Do not add to or enhance the product your customer bought
   - Require individual sign-ups for each bonus

   The problem with the last bullet point above is that your customer may not have time and/or may become slightly confused. Your original product may actually get lost in the dozens of sign up windows. Or your customer may become distracted and just decide to "close everything for later" - including the product they bought from you. This is definitely a case where less may be considered more!

2. **Testimonials, Referrals and Recommendations**
One of the best ways to build credibility is to let others do it for you.

Make it easy for your customers or clients to recommend you.

Use calls to action. Ask for referrals. This becomes easy when you make asking for referrals...
- Part of your habits and patterns
- Part of your contracts or sales agreements
- Easy - by placing a "Tell others about this product" call to action over your share buttons
- Part of your literature and presentations
- Part of your website

3. **Customer Service**
You've made the sale: Now you need to focus on follow up and customer service. Nothing destroys easily won, enthusiastic trust quite as completely as a big letdown after purchase.

We've already talked about making the product's download and utilization/implementation processes easy for your clients - but make sure you provide them with efficient, **easy options for customer service** too.

That includes helping your client or customer to...

- Easily access your site
- Find information she needs to find - quickly

- See instantly how to contact you, should she need to
- Understand how you (or your representative) will respond - and know how long she will have to wait before her issue is resolved

Outsourcing your customer service to someone who specializes in fast service and turnaround is a sensible option if you are selling many units of product or serving clients to your maximum limit.

But you need to also introduce your clients and customers to that representative - and let them know how to reach her, positioning her as your team expert. You need to help instill trust in your representative - which also boosts your own credibility.

Step Ten: Follow Up

Make sure you nurture, nourish and continue to build your reputation with your...
- Fans and followers
- Visitors and subscribers
- Customers and clients

That involves maintaining multiple online and offline platforms (e.g. social media, forums, guest speaking, workshops, and events).

It also involves planning, so there are no "gaps" in your web visibility.

It's a real relationship so treat it like one. (Think of how this would go if your subscriber were a friend you regularly interacted with, in person.)

- Give your subscribers time to check out, use, and think about your last offer.
- Be current so that fans/clients remember and care who you are.
- Provide tips, information, FAQs and answers to questions.
- Keep them up to date on new changes or products in your field.

Above all, be there and care. There's really no substitute for focusing on your customer and her needs.

Final tips for living your best life:

➤ Never forget the importance of your health and fitness... if you don't have either of these then you really have nothing – these are your most important assets

➤ Get a good night's sleep

➤ Have a no-tech bedroom

➤ Unplug earlier

➤ Take light, daily exercise

➤ Journal

➤ Meditate

- Keep the same sleep pattern

- Only sleep in bed

- Let go of things that no longer serve you – recognize, acknowledge, honor them and let them go

- Discover what is important

- Track successes

- Encourage creativity

Here's hoping you find powerful self-confidence along with your credibility to help you in your creation of a life in which you achieve your cherished dreams.

From Susie: I am so grateful to you for taking the time to choose this book for yourself or as a gift to someone you love – or both! – that I thought I would like to gift you something from my product list. I've chosen accordingly, to go with the sentiment of the book and my chapter it is entitled: **"Be Bold! Simple Steps To Building Your Confidence."**

When you lack confidence, you're putting yourself in jeopardy of losing the success you're capable of before you even begin to try.

This self-directed course guides you through the maze of building the confidence you need to get you through almost anything in life you're trying to accomplish. To download your gift, please go to: **www.tiny.cc/GiftFromSusie**.

I would also like to give you the opportunity of working with me at a special introduction rate only for readers of this book. I am offering a 30% reduction on my usual fee, so please go to **www.acercoachingassociates.com** to learn more about me and how we may work together.

Go to **www.tiny.cc/schedulewithsusie** to select a time for a 30-minute non-obligation 'Get To Know You' session (writing IAPLC into the interview time slot selected), where we will explore how we might work together.

I look forward to hearing from you:
Contact: briscoe.susie@gmail.com
www.acercoachingassociates.com
www.tiny.cc/schedulewithsusie
www.tiny.cc/GiftFromSusie

About the Author

Susie Briscoe – Founding Chair; Acer Coaching Associates
International Business, Executive, Leadership with Legacy,
Lifestyle Coach & Mentor;

#1 International Best Selling Author – "Colour Your Legacy"
Contributing author of further 6 #1 International Best Selling
books.

"Helping Business Leaders find Rainbows within their Lives"
Susie Briscoe founded **Acer Coaching Associates (ACA)** in
2004, after graduating as a fully accredited Coach, Mentor and
Supervisor with Coaching & Mentoring International
(formerly The UK College of Life Coaching), and meticulously
maintains her own CPD to remain at the cutting edge of
current best practice.

Headhunted by the Nightingale-Conant Corporation in 2008
to become their freelance Master Coach outside the US, Susie
runs her International business whilst remaining an active
Board member of: Retired Trustee: The Battersea Dogs' &
Cats' Home, 1989-2016, Patron: Church Housing Trust
(Trustee 1991-2915; Patron 2015, and the charity she founded:
Acer Foundation for Global Education & Welfare, 2006 –
present.

An enthusiastic Corporate and Executive motivator, Susie is
fervent about facilitating the developmental growth of clients

and colleagues. Susie brings a wealth of life and business experience to her Client relationships: from her 40+ years in increasingly senior roles within the Corporate, Educational, Health and Charity environment, (as well as working at Senior Director levels across a business spectrum that covers industry, commerce, academia, professional bodies and government institutions both at National and International levels) she is well used to appraising, managing people and projects, coaching/mentoring/supervising to enhance performance, implementing new programmes and facilitating learning.

She believes actions bring results: "By enabling natural talent and ability, we are able to produce outstanding results; focus, drive and enthusiasm, once released, allow us to achieve our full potential, enriching our lives and enhancing our businesses and careers." Her coaching style has been described as intuitive, empathetic, and compassionate as well as motivating. Susie has a passion for people and for making a difference by offering a supportive environment for clients. She is a strategic and lateral thinker, with proven coaching, organisational and interpersonal skills, as well as excellent leadership, team and management experience.

Since implementing her own Leadership with Legacy ideas, Susie has joyfully declared her intention of "Finding the rainbows in all those business suits. Nothing is more pleasing than to hear the delight in client's voices as they too discover their own passions." Known by some as the Conscious Breakthrough and Transitional Mentor, this all comes together with her dynamic approach to working with her clients all around the world.

"It's Time to Let Go and LIVE!!!"

By Carolyn R Owens

Many people go through life having chosen a career path that someone else planned for them. They have little or no passion about their work and choose to just go through the motions. They go to work, come home, go to work, come home, go to work. You get the picture. They chose a life of mediocrity. It can become so routine, they are not able to see the pattern they have created. It's as if they have become a robot, just existing. This is not living.

Throughout their life they are searching for happiness in a career someone else wanted for them. Is this you? Did your mom or dad or maybe even your school counselor convince you to go into what they saw as the "perfect" career field for you? You went to the college they wanted you to, not realizing the whole time you were feeling miserable while struggling to get through the courses. However, you did not want to disappoint them, so you just kept going and going.

Or maybe you just took the first job that came along and stuck with it. You worked your way up in the company, and you have so much to be proud about. But you are not excited about the work you do. You feel obligated to stay because of all the company has done for you over the years. So, you just keep sticking it out.

If you are a business owner, maybe you knew exactly what type of business you wanted to start. You told everyone and invested a lot of money getting started. But, after a few years, the business just isn't what you thought it would be. Life has changed. Your interest has changed. Maybe even your values have changed. However, if you switch gears after all the work, time and money you invested, you will disappoint a lot of people. You will be a failure.

As time goes by, one day you pause and take a good hard look in the mirror, but you can't even find yourself. You ask yourself, "How did I end up here?" If you pull back the curtain and begin to dissect your life, you can see how much a career choice plays a role in the joy, fulfillment and happiness one experiences in life.

Are you living the life YOU truly desire to live or are you living a life someone else created for you? Are you feeling as if you must stay on the path you are on and someday, whenever that might be, you can do what you really want to do? But what if you didn't have to wait? You can learn to let go, start living and create the life YOU want to live. If you think it's impossible, the first thing you need to do is look once again in the mirror and tell yourself "I'm possible."

The job or career path you choose is meant to empower you to have and do all you want to in life. If you chose the wrong career path, you can end up just existing. But as Confucius said, "Choose a job you love, and you will never have to work a day in your life."

Most of us spend our school years preparing how to make a living as opposed to how to create a life. It's easy to lose sight of what we value most in our lives. Society teaches us we must live a certain way, or have certain things, in order to be considered successful. So much so, your vision can be a bit blurry when it comes to what you really want.

Creating the life you desire is a journey. A journey faced with obstacles, winding roads and sometimes, a fork in the road.

You will have to make choices. Some will come naturally and easy for you. With other choices, you'll spend time thinking about what's best at this given time versus what you want right now.

In working with clients as a Career Strategist, Leadership and Life Coach, and through my personal experience, I have found there are common points most people will encounter along the path. Some, I would dare say, are even necessary to succeed. If you are ready to create the life you truly desire, here are a few things you need to consider as you begin your journey.

Know what you want.
Knowing what you want is just that -- knowing what YOU want. Notice the emphasis on you. It is important to understand, this is not what someone else wants for you, but the life you truly want to live.

In order to know what you want, ask yourself two questions:
- What do you want to get out of life? and
- What do you want to give back to life?

Answering these questions will lead you to knowing what you want to become, what you want to own, how you want to give back, and what legacy you want to leave behind.

To fully understand what you want out of life, you must first identify what you value. You must spend time thinking about it and writing down what you value in life, both personally and professionally. If you really want to be happy, live a fulfilling life, and work at a meaningful career, you must both know **and** be in alignment with your values.

Know what you value.

Too often I have coached a client through a values exercise only to discover personal conflicts they were not aware of. They tell me what they value most in life but realize they invest little or no time in these areas. Through the coaching process, they are able to identify what has been causing them to feel so unhappy and empty. They learn what they need to let go of.

Knowing what you value is a very important key, if not the most important, in creating a life you desire. However, it is often a step along the journey that is overlooked. As I find this to be the most important step, I will spend a little more time on this area.

A value is something that makes you happy. Most people don't know what truly makes them happy. Whether we realize it or not, our values influence our behaviors, choices and emotions. They influence our habits, our lifestyles, and our way of being and interacting with the world. Don't confuse values with your beliefs, which come from your head. Values come from the heart.

A value is something that, at this moment in time, you feel strongly about, and you should not compromise it for anything. You may have 20 or 30 values but there are only about 6 - 8 that make up 90% of your happiness. When you live life in conflict with your values you tend to be stressed out and unhappy.

As you grow and experience life, your values can and do change. You aren't obligated to stick with the same values for your entire life. What you valued in your 20's, before you landed that dream job, before you had a spouse, before you had children, can change. However, you should be pausing along your journey to assess and see if and how they have changed. If you are not honoring them by truly making them a priority, you can't and won't ever be truly happy.

When you are not living in alignment with your values, you are merely existing, going through the motions day in and day out. You are not living up to your full potential. This is not how you should live. Life should be full of joy, full of passion. If you value simplicity and you're living with clutter and disorganization, you won't be happy.

If you value financial freedom and you're are living in debt, you won't be happy.

If family is something you value and you're in a career that does not allow you to spend much time with your family, guess what? You won't be happy.

Writing is something I love to do, and there was a time when I wasn't making it a priority in my life. It was one of those things I said I love to do, but I wasn't doing it. I was doing the things I felt I "needed" to do, but not the things I was passionate about. How about you? Do you talk about what's important to you, but if you took a good look, you would find you are not doing those things? We talk about the priorities in our lives, but are we really treating them like a priority? We tend to put these things on the back burner, making excuses on why we can't do them.

The unhappiness created carries over to your career and/or business. If you want to find joy in your life and career, you must know what your values are AND work hard to live in alignment with them.

Identify goals and develop an action plan.
Once you have clarified what you value in life and how you want to design your life, you must identify goals and an

action plan that will get you there. The plan you develop will serve as your roadmap along the journey.

As with your values and desires in life, the goals you decide upon are YOUR goals. There may be others around you who want a seat at the boardroom table or to have a million-dollar company. This doesn't have to be you. Whatever your goals may be, they represent the life you want to live and the legacy you want to leave behind.

Your goals should be S.M.A.R.T. – specific, measurable, actionable, relevant and timely. I recommend you focus on no more than three goals at a time. When you have too many goals, it's hard to focus on all of them. You end up getting very little accomplished. Have three overarching goals and as you complete one, you can add a new one to the list.

With your goals, you want to develop action steps. What specific steps do you need to take to achieve the goals? From the overarching three goals you identified, you can develop a subset of monthly goals with weekly and/or daily actions steps. Know that there is no set rule on how this should be done. You must find what method works best for you.

You may find that in order to achieve your goal, you need additional training, especially if you are going into a whole new career or industry. You may have to spend time working in a position you don't like while you build a foundation in the new area. Do not let things like this discourage you! Always look at it from the positive side. Every step forward will get you closer to the life you truly desire.

As you can accomplish your goals, be sure to celebrate along the way. We focus so much on the negative things that happen in life, that we don't highlight the "wins" enough. Celebrate and have fun throughout the journey.

Define what success looks like for YOU.

Success means different things to different people. I almost lost sight of this when I was establishing my business, Infinity Coaching, Inc. There were so many people telling me what I should be doing. So much so that it was clouding the way for me to create the business I wanted to have.

I had someone go so far as to say, if I didn't do exactly what he said, my business would fail. I think it would have been the other way around. Had I done what he said, my business would have definitely failed.

As I began to define success according to my terms, my business started growing. I learned to play by the rules I set and was able to build a business I am proud of.

Be it in your life, career or business, know what success looks like for YOU. If you are the parent of a toddler, success may look different for you now than when your child becomes a teenager. If you are working a full-time job and starting a business, you may need to continue working that job until you can transition according to the rules you set.

This quote by former co-chair of Disney Media Networks and Disney/ABC Television Group president, Anne Sweeny sums it up perfectly, "Define success on your own terms, achieve it by your own rules, and build a life you are proud to live."

Raise your self-awareness.

Having assessed and determined how we want to live our lives, we can now work towards achieving this lifestyle. In order to do that, we must begin to raise our self-awareness. When we begin to live in the moment, knowing who we are and what we desire, we begin to live an authentic life. A life "true" to ourselves and others we interact with.

Self-awareness is about being able to look at ourselves in the mirror and face the good and the bad. It's about acknowledging our strengths and weaknesses. It's about accepting what we can't and aren't willing to change. Until we can fully accept and acknowledge who we are and who we really want to be, we will not reach our full potential, nor will we live and love authentically.

As we begin to learn who we really are, it will impact all areas of our lives. We stop doing the things that everyone else wants us to do, and we start living. The landscape of our life changes.

When we fully embrace ourselves, we understand we get to choose. We have a choice on how we show up every day. We can appreciate ourselves for who we really are. There is no longer a need to seek approval from everyone else. We realize and understand we are not perfect.

Embrace your fear.
Everything you have done to create the life your desire, can be blown away by the strong winds of fear. Fear can have one believe in things that will hold them prisoner in an imaginary cell. In order to move past it, you must learn to embrace the fear and make fear your friend.

Lisa (the names are fictitious but the story all too real) was getting ready to go to an interview when her best friend Stephanie called her to wish her well. The position she was being considered for would be a promotion in her current department. Stephanie told her good luck, and they chatted for a bit, but then Stephanie asked, "Are you sure you're ready for this?" Lisa asked what she meant, and Stephanie went on to explain.

"I mean, when you take this job, your life is going to change. Sure, it's more money, but is it worth it? I remember a few days ago when you were having a bad day. If you get the job, you'll probably have even more bad days. Plus, you are going to be the first woman who serves in this position. You're so shy. I just worry how you will handle it all." Lisa told Stephanie she could handle the job and it would all be great.

On her way to the interview, Lisa started thinking, maybe Stephanie is right. I mean my mom always told me, I shouldn't take my luck for granted. Once you have a good thing that works, you should just stick with it. I wasn't meant to go too far. Maybe they are both right. They wouldn't say if they didn't know me best.

Lisa let fear and self-doubt enter her mind and she didn't show up for the interview. It created an uncomfortable situation at work, so she decided to look for a new job. She ended up taking a position with a lower salary for the same amount of work.

Fear can cause us not to believe in ourselves enough. It shows up for business owners as well. Many people will start down the path of entrepreneurship and quit. What they don't realize is, far too many times, if they had held on just one more day, the sale they were waiting for was on its way.

Fear can cause us to stay stuck in a career, life or business we no longer want to be in. We get caught up in what others think, how we will be judged, self-doubt, insecurity and so much more. How many opportunities have you let pass you by because of fear? Most of the time the thing we fear, never happens. In the words of French essayist, Michel de Montaigne, "My life has been full of terrible misfortunes most of which never happened."

If you think you can eliminate fear, you can't. It will find you along your journey and try to blow you off your path. When you see it coming your way, ask yourself how important is your goal to you? What is life going to be like if you quit? Not taking action can often be more painful then failing. You don't want to be the person who looks back full of regret because of all the things you didn't do.

Another way to embrace your fear is to prepare for the fear before it arrives.

Assess the outcomes.
When developing a plan to create a life you truly desire, you can assess different outcomes in order to be prepared for obstacles along the way. You do this by asking yourself the question – What's the worst thing that could really happen?

Put it all on the table so you know what it is. There will be people who won't appreciate your journey. They will laugh at your dreams. They will laugh at your goals. Your friends, family members, the people you thought who believed in you the most, may not support you. Is this something you can handle?

When I retired from the military, I was offered a very great opportunity to work within the federal government. The starting offer was unbelievable. Even so, I turned it down. My father who had retired from working as a civil servant, was infuriated with me. He told me I had to take the position. His exact words were "Do you understand me?" I told him, "Dad. I love you, but I have to go now." This was during my first year of business.

My father wasn't the only one who told me, this (my business) wasn't for me. My father passed away before he could see the outcome, but my friends have gained even more respect for me for holding my ground and sticking with it.

Once you have an idea of the worst thing that can happen, ask yourself the following questions:

- If it happens can you get over it?
- Is it going to be that detrimental to you, that you are not willing to take the risk?
- What would it feel like if you didn't try?
- If it does happen, are you able to have a back up plan in place? Can you move on to the next goal or next project?
- What if this never happens and everything goes right?

Don't go into it thinking, "I'm going to fail." Step out of your comfort zone and go for it.

We will face many obstacles along the journey of life, but we have a choice: either to not try, to quit, or to find a way around the obstacle. You must decide how bad you really want to fulfill your dream. Are you ready to move past the coulda's and maybe's, and create what you desire? If so, tell yourself, "I'm going for it, I'm not afraid, but if this does happen, I have a backup plan."

Choose to play and live life to the fullest – It's worth it!

You don't have to go it alone
Creating your best life, the life you truly desire sounds good, but it can be difficult. We often don't want to face ourselves in the mirror. We don't want to hear the difficult questions we may have to answer. When we don't like our answers, we can easily default back to our routine mode. We go back to being a robot that just exists. This isn't the life we want, but we have become so comfortable with this way of living it's hard to see

anything else is possible. You don't have to go it alone. A Life Coach can accompany and assist you along the journey.

I am a true believer in the coaching process. Not just because I serve as a coach, but because of all the success stories I have seen, studied and continue to hear about. Coaches are there to support their clients in achieving their goals. Unlike family and friends, they do not have a personal agenda when it comes to the outcome.

The right coach will motivate, inspire and lift you up. They will provide you with skills and strategies that will help you move past fear, so you can get a seat at the boardroom table, grow your business, or get the promotion you always wanted. When we talk about creating the career, business, or life you truly desire, here are some of the ways you can benefit from working with a life coach.

Benefits of working with a life coach:
   Assessing YOUR values.
   When it comes to identifying what you value and want in life, it can be hard to get rid of the noise in your head. You can easily start to think of all the reasons why you can't have the life you desire. You end up getting in your own way before you even start the journey. Like Lisa, who we discussed early in the chapter, you can allow the thoughts of others, what your parents, friends or family members say, keep you from the life you want to have.

   A coach can assist you with moving past the limiting beliefs and mental roadblocks you have created. You can learn how to quiet the negative thoughts you tell yourself. You can develop strategies for when those thoughts resurface, so you can continue the journey and not quit.

Keep in mind that these are your values and not your coach's values. You should not look to them to identify your values for you.

Setting goals.
When it comes to setting goals, coaches know the right questions to ask. They can help you determine if your goals are relevant for what you want to accomplish. If the goals are relevant, they can help you assess if this is the right time for you to work on the goals.

During the journey it may seem as if, with the goals you set, you won't ever be able to create your dream life. It doesn't mean you have to give up on your dream. It may mean you just have to develop new goals. Your coach will walk you through a process to understand why the goals did not align with your vision and what new goals you need to set to get back on track.

Moving past fear.
Have you ever heard someone say, "I'm not afraid of anything." I would bet there is something they're afraid of. The difference becomes how they handle fear. If you don't embrace it, fear will trap you from ever creating the life you desire to have.

One of the main reasons is that we are afraid to fail. So afraid, we don't even try. You must develop the courage to move past the fear and take risks. A life coach can provide encouragement, support, and will believe in you even when you don't believe in yourself.

Working together, each obstacle or roadblock you face will be a learning opportunity. From the experience you will grow and raise your self-awareness. You will adjust your plan and find different ways to achieve your goals, even if it means changing your goals.

When it comes to fear of failure, always keep in mind what Robert H. Schuller, American Christian televangelist, pastor, motivational speaker, and author said. "Failure doesn't mean you are a failure, it just means you haven't succeeded yet."

Your coach will be there to help you get back up, dust yourself off and start back on YOUR journey.

Developing your roadmap.
When looking to achieve something in life, many people will write down goals and that's it. They do not take the time to write out the action steps they need to take to achieve the goals. Some people want to rush through the process and jump right in. They end up taking the long way when they could have taken a much shorter route. This is where your coach can help you.

Working with a coach, you can clearly identify what steps need to be taken and when they should be done. They can assist you with identifying the resources needed and where you can find them. A coach will help you prioritize your steps, so you don't veer off onto a dead-end street.

Accountability.
One of the biggest obstacles that gets in the way of creating the life you desire is, drumroll please – YOU!!! You can identify your values, write out your goals, write out your action steps, and even reduce the fear you feel. But if you don't do one thing, you will never

have what you desire, and I do mean never. What is that one thing? You must implement everything you have planned by taking action.

Sounds simple doesn't it? Just take action. It sounds simple but so many people don't do it. They may take a few steps along the path but then they stop. They can give you all the reasons why, but what are those reasons really? They are excuses.

Family and friends often accept the excuses you give. Sometimes they even fuel the flame by agreeing with all the reasons why you can't do something. They tell you, don't worry you can do it tomorrow. Tomorrow they tell you the same thing and before you know it, you're right back on the cycle you were trying to free yourself from.

The path along the journey may get a little bumpy. There will be things that come up you have no control over. These "things" will make you want to stop, sit down and forget the destination you were heading to. That destination was your life. The life you have been dreaming of.

A coach can provide support along the journey by helping you figure out the real reasons why you stopped. Have you found out that the path you are on isn't really the road you want to take? That's okay. Your coach can work with you to find the path you really want to be on. Are you not doing the steps you outlined in your plan? Your coach can help you identify why you're stuck and help you move forward so you can continue YOUR journey.

A coach can help you answer the tough questions you don't really want to answer. You can work through whatever is holding you back, so you can create the life you desire. They do this by encouraging you, supporting you, but most importantly, holding you accountable.

In this book you get to learn about creating the life, business or career you desire from highly skilled and trained coaches. Each coach presents a unique approach to coaching, but all know the impact it can have on your life. Take your time to read and digest each chapter. Try a few of the strategies and see what works for you.

The "True" reflection in the mirror.
Remember the mirror I mentioned before? I want you to go look in that mirror and face yourself. This time you are going to find your True self. Take a look in the mirror and ask yourself three questions:

1- "What is the life, career or business I want to have?"
2- "What's holding me back from creating this for ME?"

Before you answer the third question close your eyes. I want you to not only say the answer, but see it. See what this really looks like for you.

The third question is:
3- "What would my life be like if I was truly living the life I want to live?"

Now what are you going to do to make it happen? It's time for you to define success on YOUR own terms. Don't live the life someone else has designed for you; build a life YOU are proud to live.

If you would like to learn more about the services or programs I offer or if I can be of assistance to you along your journey, please reach out to me at cowens@infinitycoaching.net. Don't be afraid to take a chance – the reward is much greater than the risk. *Here's to your success!*

About the Author

Carolyn R Owens, PCC, CPC, SPHR
Certified Career Strategist, Leadership and Life Coach
www.infinitycoaching.net
cowens@infinitycoaching.net

Carolyn R. Owens is a retired United States Navy Commander, Amazon #1 Best Selling Author and President and Founder of Infinity Coaching, Inc. A leading authority on leadership and professional development, Carolyn uses principles derived from the world's most respected military training programs to educate and train top leaders and business owners across the globe. She works with her clients to awaken their self-awareness, so they can achieve greater communication, interaction and engagement with their customers, clients and teams as well as in their personal relationships.

During her military career, she served as the Director of Human Capital Management for an organization of over 4,800 civilian, military and contract personnel. Her favorite assignment was when she served as a Professor in the Department of Command Leadership and Management at the United States Army War College. Upon retiring from the military, she decided to turn the part she loved most into a second career and Infinity Coaching, Inc. was born.

Carolyn served as the President of the Maryland Career Development Association and is the host of the podcast, "Let's Coach". She has been featured in Money Magazine, Fox News Magazine, Huffington Post, YourTango, Legacy in the Making Magazine, and many other publications. She serves as a guest speaker for conferences, seminars and virtual events, which has included the American Psychological Association (APA) Career Fair, Maryland Counseling Association and Ultimate Woman Network Conference. She is a frequent guest expert on local and national radio shows.

Having served in key leadership positions and as a successful business owner, Carolyn knows quite well some of the challenges one faces when pursuing the career and life of their dreams. The company she founded, Infinity Coaching, Inc., provides career, executive and leadership coaching that moves individuals forward, allowing them to take COMMAND of their lives.

To raise your awareness about your leadership skills, visit **http://leadershipmasteryassessment.com/** for a free assessment. You will quickly discover areas you are performing well in as well as areas that may need additional attention. This will enable you to clearly define your goals and achieve a life you truly desire. It's all about having success on YOUR own terms!

Connect with Carolyn on social media:

Twitter: https://www.twitter.com/CarolROwens
LinkedIn:
https://www.linkedin.com/in/cowensinfinitycoaching/
Facebook: https://www.facebook.com/infinitycoaching.co/
Instagram: https://www.instagram.com/carolynrowens/

"Bridging The Gaps with Mantra, a Spiritual Celebration"

By Sylvia Snyder, MA, BA, CHt, CNHP, Non-denominational Clergy

Overview

"Don't let not knowing how it'll end keep you from beginning. Uncertainty chases us out into the open where life's true magic is waiting." - Angel Chernoff

Everything I ever asked for, the Universe has given me, and it all came by using what I am going to share with you in this article. I tried so many ways to manifest my intentions, with no luck...until I applied material from Thomas Ashley-Farrand, "Mantra Sacred Words of Power" (1999, Sounds True, CD) and attended a veteran women's group for Post-Traumatic Stress Disorder.

In 2009, I woke up around 3am, turned the TV on, and did not like what was on. So I started looking through some material from my 8-week veteran women's group for Post-Traumatic Stress Disorder (PTSD). The leader of the group had material on Mindfulness. She demonstrated how Mindfulness can be helpful with changing your thoughts, and managing negative information for positive change. In her material, there was a lot of resource information, which seemed valuable. So I started to browse the Internet looking for more information on Mindfulness. I realized the veteran women's group had helped me to relax and to begin to stay in present moments with reduced distressing thoughts.

Somehow I came across "Mantra Sacred Words of Power" by Thomas Ashley-Farrand. Listening to his material, I instantly, felt impact. It was awesome. I ordered anything and everything with his name on it. Hearing his tapes, reading his books, along with attending the veteran women's group guided me to a spiritual mode of living that continues to the present day. Now, although I no longer attend the veteran women's group, I continue using information from Thomas Ashley-Farrand.

Fundamentals

My program, "Bridging the Gaps with Mantra, a Spiritual Celebration," is a facilitator for understanding yourself better, even while undergoing an experience that can be perceived as overwhelming. The facilitating process for me was using mantras (words that through their repetition produce specific sounds and vibrations) as a meditation technique to quiet my inner self-talk. I was able to lessen my self-talk to a point where I actuality recognized an "inner present moment" stance. My use of mantra meditating techniques had resulted in clearness, inner stillness, and a reduction of stress and anxiety. I had finally realized my meditation stance and the process of being in a calmness state. My meditation and calmness stance are part of my configuration on this journey of crafting a system that creates more present-moment awareness and a longer grounded stance.

Jonathan and Andi Goldman report, "Sound can heal the body, mind, and spirit, as well as the emotions. Through this interrelationship of sound and self, we can balance and harmonize any of these aspects within ourselves and affect all parts of our being."

Basic mantras are energy field-based sounds that:
> (1) Will help create a translucent, and peaceful stance of the mind to promote a greater awareness, and
> (2) Will help with staying focused and centered to complete any task.

When you know yourself better, you can create a reality that can have a positive undertone and a good temperament for success.

Dr. Galina Merline, a physicist, researcher, and developer in the field of sound waves, states, "The human body is a radiant machine. Every living element in our body radiates. Our brain operates on electrical current, our ears absorb sound vibrations, and we produce voices and temperature (sic)." For most of us, our ego struggles with letting go and allowing new data to come in for change. Therefore, developing the mindset to be open, when looking into the unknown, is a significant step in getting rid of outdated personal data that no longer works.

What to Expect
The process is not complex, or hard to do; however, being consistent with taking time to practice is extremely important. Everything you need you already have---it just needs to be awakened. Initially, the conscious and subconscious minds are the focus. The process can be slow moving and sluggish due to the course of using ordinary encounters with the conscious mind and subconscious mind. But it is effective in lifting the veil to uncover events that have not been dealt with on a conscious level. It does not have to be a traumatic event, but the situation just needs to be special to you. To bring a special situation out into the conscious mind format takes time and work to sustain a balanced energy field.

The Thomas Ashely-Farrand report on the effects of sound is believed to have Hindu and Buddhist beginnings. But mention also can be found in the New Testament. The Gospel of John, states "in the beginning was the word…"Note here that light is not the beginning: instead, God creates the phenomenon by speaking it, "And God said, let there be light." The primary mechanism in creation is sound. When I read this, it did not match what I was taught in church as a child. I recall the Preacher citing "Let there be light" as the beginning of Religion, (Southern Baptist Spirituality).

There was a huge change in my worldview from what I was taught as a child to what I was learning as an adult. What I now see is that mantra songs are not about religion, but rather spirituality. It was the small particulars of old knowledge that I had to let go of, to make space for new data toward spiritual relations with myself and others. Acquiring an understanding of meditating techniques and finding the right mantra was the beginning of my clear and calm mindset. That mindset let me obtain and maintain support for quiet awareness, an essential element of a meditative state.

Individualizing Mantras

While in the hospital with my mother, in the middle of May 2017, I received a call from a family member experiencing a personal problem. Earlier that morning, I had texted one seed mantra, and a mantra song for her to meditate on. The process for her was to relax the inner-self and prepare the mind, body, and spirit for what is to come: inner quietness. I explained to her that, when you listen to mantra songs, the sounds from the words vibrate, dislodging any energy stuck on the chakras that's preventing them from moving freely. According to Amazingliferesources.com, a mantra is a "sound or a word that is being repeated frequently in the mind or out loud, and that results in silencing the constant noise and chatter of your thoughts" (Free-eBooks.net, 2016).

I also described to her, another process to sustain her "intent" before, during, and after the meditation procedure. To accomplish this, I prepared some information on how the process should work. It was broken down into the simplest form for her, due to her being in such a crisis state. I emphasized the need to allow herself to express feelings, because emotional release is an important component in peeling away negative blockage surrounding your intention.

The family member called later that morning reporting feeling better, and that she had received an email notifying her of a job interview with a federal organization. She had the interview, and later that month received a call from their Human Resource department that she had the job.

Using Mantra songs, according to Ashely-Farrand, helps to heal negative experiences. From reading him, I learned that having uncertainty about how to manage some situations creates anxiety, fear, anger, and sadness centered around wanting a positive result from the encounter but not sure how to go about getting that result. Before knowing this, I had no positive outcome from difficult situations because I was trying to work through the experience while holding on to all the above-mentioned emotions. I was clutching onto a specific outcome, and thus blocking any chance of positive change in the situation. I had no strategic design to get from where I was in the experience to where I wanted the experience to go.

Now, when I have an incident of unmanageable negative energy, I center myself with the seed mantra OM, followed by OM GUM GHANAPATAYEI SWAHA, mantra song.

I am an adult child of an alcoholic, and I have "adult child" traits. Adultchildren.org was founded on the belief that family dysfunction is a disease that infects children and also affects them later as adults. Utilizing mantra techniques when my adult child traits surfaced (with sabotaging intentions), has helped me to understand:

(1) What is happening with my emotions when they resurface,
(2) The importance of taking time to learn how to quiet my inner negative self-talk,
(3) In this instance "sitting on my hands" can be productive (Cambridge Academic Content Dictionary states, "sitting on your hands is to do nothing about a problem, or a situation that needs dealing with.")
(4) The importance of learning internal signs of acceptance when this awareness takes place, and
(5) Not to allow personal trauma recall to get in the way of being in the present moment.

I genuinely, believe that use of frequencies and vibrational practice can assist individuals going through any circumstances.

Self-Compassion

Self-compassion is a factor to consider in creating the groundwork for meditative techniques. It helps to be more sympathetic with yourself when feelings reemerge that are linked to shortcomings, blunders, disappointments, and dreadful circumstances. Self-compassion allows inner self-talk to set the stage for acceptance of self by reducing faultfinding or nit-picking episodes.

With your focus on **how** you want to increase your ability to stay grounded, practicing self-compassion allows you a moment to review a thought in order to choose loving kindness instead of beating yourself up for past experiences. Being grounded and having self-compassion are keys in sustaining steadfastness. With these two keys, you can accomplish your intent by tying a knot and hanging the hell on, in the mist of personal change.

Kristin Neff states, "From the Buddhist point of view, you have to care about yourself before you can really care about other people. If you are continually judging and criticizing yourself while trying to be kind to others, you are drawing artificial boundaries and distinctions that only lead to feelings of separation and isolation. This is the opposite of oneness, interconnection, and universal love — the ultimate goal of most spiritual paths, no matter which tradition."

Reformation

If you are at an intersection in your life, and you do not know which path to take, "Bridging, the Gaps with Mantras, a Spiritual Celebration" is the syllabus for you. The program is a self-paced, personal enhancement, educational proposal created on the notion that personal success and pleasure in the end come from self-improved perceptiveness. This program provides essential steps and strategies on how to move from negative self-perceptions to a healthier self-awareness in the direction of goal success. The techniques are helpful in reestablishing clarity, stability, direction, inner harmony, and self-compassion.

Assumption

"Bridging the Gaps with Mantra, a Spiritual Celebration" is an awareness program of clarification. In the program's progression you strengthen your self-responsibility. Self-responsibility points toward less detachment from yourself and others; swift rejoining when you do detach; better responsiveness of love; motivation and capacity to spread love externally; and inclination to truly scrutinize your share in any dispute. Herbert Harris states, "The key to a successful life is to realize that living is a learned habit, an acquired skill."

I also discovered that it is not difficult to manifest my desires after improving my self-responsibility.

My celebration consists of:
(1) Letting go of old negative habits used during childhood;
(2) Cultivating healthy perceptions to flourish into emotional truths from restored notions, opinions, and interpretations;
(3) Working through uncomfortable feelings to permit unknown positive outcomes to be aired with no interruption; and
(4) Acceptance of my voyage of discovery through distressing emotions, which proved a worthy climb into unfamiliar space that needed strong commitment, but feeling gratified about the spiritual walk.

My coaching services will help you:
- Live a life according to your dreams and wants.
- Formulate better choices that feel right for you.
- Construct emboldening visualizations for healthier outcomes.
- Generate intentions that stimulate and inspire you.
- Offer an educational curriculum on Subtle Energy Bodies, Meditation, Mindfulness, Mantra Songs, Self-Concept, and the Chakra System.

DISCLAIMER
The coaching services provided by Sylvia Snyder, Professional Life Coach are not medical or psychiatric treatments, are not intended to diagnose or treat any medical conditions, and should not be used as a replacement for treatment of disease or illness as provided by a licensed medical practitioner. Please consult your healthcare provider if you have any medical concerns or questions.

Bibliography

1. Ashely-Farrand, T. (1999). Sounds True | Publisher of book, audio, and video titles in the fields of self-development, personal growth, and spirituality. Retrieved from https://www.udemy.com/user/soundstrue/
2. Goldman, J., & Goldman, A. (2011) (p. 1). Chakra frequencies: Tantra of sound. Rochester, VT: Destiny Books.
3. Merline, Galina, G. M. (2018, July 18). PsyMinds, Retrieved December 12, 2018, from https://psy-minds.com/frequency-human-body/
4. Neff, Kristin. Self-Compassion (p. 7). HarperCollins e-books. Kindle Edition.

About the Author

Sylvia Snyder: (65 years old), is a Professional Coach who help clients identify personal or professional intentions and generate strategies for successful manifestation using mantras, frequencies and vibration, meditating techniques, and mindfulness. The approaches used with clients, are the ones I use in my personal and professional life with really great results. I started my coaching business in 2012, to continue helping men and women (veterans and civilian population) with indications of substance abuse and Post-Traumatic Stress Disorder become more successful in creating the best intent in order to have a positive experience through manifesting wholesome goal.

Prior to retirement, I served 14 1/2 years in the US Army a Substance Abuse Counselor with honorable discharge, acquired a Bachelor and Master-of-Arts degree, Certified Hypnotherapy Therapist, Certified Natural Health Practitioner, Professional Coach., Non-denominational Clergy. Currently, I have a wide range of programs and services-from individual and group coaching, to seminars and keynote speeches.

To contact Sylvia, go to: https://www.esteemedknack.com Or email: info@esteemedknack.com

"Live the Life You Want"

By Jeannette Koczela

How do you create the life you want? As a spiritual life coach, I want to suggest that you start by *living* the life you want. What do I mean by that? I mean, that you don't have to wait for the life you want---you can begin living it right now. Here are some steps you can take to live the life you want while you're in the process of creating it.

1- Imagine it first.
You can start living the life you want by imagining it. It is a matter of vision. How do you envision your future? What do you want to accomplish? You must be able to imagine yourself doing what you want to do, and being the person you need to be in order to do that thing. If you can picture yourself as a winner, it's easier to become one.

If you have trouble imagining your own future, find someone who is already doing what you want to do and imagine what it's like for them. You may even want to contact that person and ask them what it's like, telling them that you aspire to be like them. Or you may have a coach who can help you.

Then take some minutes every day to imagine yourself living the life you want to create. This will give your brain a way to focus on your desired outcome in order to activate the energy around the fulfillment of your dreams. As we've all heard (but so easily forget!)---what you think about most is what you will get.

Even athletes are known to successfully use imagining techniques to prepare for winning events and breaking records.

Everyone has an imagination, and you have free and unlimited use of it, so put it to work!

2- Get your emotions involved

When you visualize your life happening the way you want it to, get as many of your senses involved as you can. Feel the excitement, the joy, the sense of accomplishment as well as how it looks, sounds, and smells. The more senses you activate, the better.

We all know that advertisers use words to arouse our emotions. That's because they know that it's human nature to first decide on purchasing something with our emotions and only then justify it with our rational minds. In the same way, you can use your own human nature to "sell" yourself on the idea that you are manifesting the life you want by getting your emotions involved in your visualization.

3- Ask the right questions.

Tony Robbins, probably the one life coach that everyone has heard of, and author of "Unlimited Power" and "Awaken the Giant Within," says that the difference between successful and unsuccessful people is in the questions they ask themselves. People who are successful ask "empowering" questions, and people who are not, ask "non-empowering" questions.

Here are some examples of non-empowering questions:
- Why is this (awful thing) happening to me?
- Why can't I make this (good thing) happen?
- What if I can't do this?
- Why does this always happen to me?
- Why can't I {fill in the blank}?

Once you become aware of the non-empowering questions you are asking, you can substitute more empowering questions such as…

- What can I learn from this situation?
- What do I need in order to make this happen?
- How can I {fill in the blank}?

These kinds of questions stimulate your brain to come up with solutions and remind your brain of all the resources you have available to you. When you ask your brain the right questions, you will get answers that are more meaningful and appropriate for reaching your goals.

Your amazing brain can locate answers to just about anything, especially if it's about yourself, such as who you are and what you are destined to do. But if you are constantly asking the wrong questions, you are not going to get very far in life or accomplish your goals with joy and ease.

You have the power to overcome any obstacle in your life if you just ask the right questions.

4- Believe in yourself

You may remember Wayne Dyer turning around the old adage, "I'll believe it when I see it" to "You'll see it when you believe it." This is so true! You've first got to believe that you can do it---that you have what it takes. Of course, that's one reason why people hire a coach---sometimes we need someone with an objective viewpoint to give us encouragement.

You not only need to believe in yourself and your ability to accomplish your dreams, but you also need to make goals that are realistic and therefore believable.

A coach can also help you make sure that the goal that you want to accomplish is realistic. If it isn't, they can give you guidance on how to make it clearer, more appropriate for your talents and skills, and/or more realistic from a time point of view. For example, maybe you have a realistic goal, but the amount of time you thought was necessary to accomplish it wasn't realistic. Adjusting the time frame can make the goal more realistic and believable.

Ultimately, you need to have enough self-confidence and self-esteem to believe that your goal is not only possible, but also that you are capable of achieving it. Some people doubt themselves because they don't know how they will accomplish their goal. But actually the "how" comes along after---and in a way results from---the belief and conviction that you are going to do it.

A coach can help you develop the confidence you need to believe in yourself and to accomplish what you desire, whether it's a career change, a relationship issue, or a business-building endeavor.

Of course, your belief in yourself is not the whole ball of wax. You can't just believe something and wait for it to happen. You must take action in the direction of the goal. As with any goal or dream, you need to find out what you need to know to accomplish it. You may need to hone your current skills or acquire new ones. But your belief will carry you over the rough spots.

5- Journal your way to the life you want.
One helpful tool for creating the life you want that is often overlooked is journaling. Writing down your thoughts and feelings, as well as your goals and dreams, makes them more solidified in your awareness.

The act of handwriting (or even typing) is a kinesthetic action. And we know from the field of psychology, that kinesthetic actions help make stronger impressions in your brain. If you do those actions often, it's like creating a pathway (literally a pathway of neurons) in the brain to your desired goal.

Sometimes just by writing out your thoughts when you hit a snag or roadblock, can help you can work out a solution that you may not have come up with just by thinking about it. Seeing it on paper (or on screen) can bring greater clarity to your situation.

Journaling is a wonderful way to let your imagination come up with ideas you may not have thought of, or thought of but not remembered to write down in the hustle-bustle of the daily tasks. It's also a time for self, for silence and reflection and this may be a gift you need to give yourself periodically or regularly in order to handle life.

6- Alter your course when it's off.
When a plane or spacecraft gets off of its trajectory or path, it must be put back on the right path. That's called a course-correction. According to an entry on the Northwestern University website, "The location of the spacecraft is determined and its course vector (the speed and direction of its flight) is calculated. This is then compared with the path it *should* be on. A new vector is computed that will put it back on course. The ship's attitude thrusters aim the ship, and the main thruster pushes it along the adjusted path."

Like that, to live an enriching, fulfilling life, we need to hone our ability to course-correct. When you see that an error has been made, or something isn't going "in the right direction", you must assess where you are, review where you're headed, and make the necessary adjustments to keep moving forward.

To err is human; therefore, one of the most important skills we can develop is course correction. Sometimes, life is like a test and we choose the wrong answer. When that happens, it's sometimes easiest to just get up the next day and do the same thing over again, hoping it will turn out better.

But life is an evolutionary progression that involves constant change, and requires constant adaptation. We try something, we test it, tweak it, make more changes, and adapt it in order to make it work.

7- Boosts along the way

Recognize the ways that you are already living the life you want to create. Sometimes we are so focused on the end goal, that we fail to acknowledge the small wins. As you travel on your life journey, you need to give yourself a pat on the back for small wins, as well as celebrate the bigger milestones.

It's good to keep your attention on your ultimate goal, but not at the expense of the enjoyment of the journey. Plan out a few ways to celebrate when something goes well! Feeling grateful and joyous for even the smallest positive events in your life attracts more of them to you. As you grow in your personal development, and spend more attention on what is going well, you will start attracting larger wins.

8-Dream Bigger

Make sure your dream is big enough. Sometimes we lose the spark that set us going on a quest to a goal because the goal wasn't big enough to maintain the excitement, drive, and tenacity to keep going. Your goal should be big enough to make you enthusiastically start each day, eager to begin working on that exciting goal. You have been put on this earth with amazing capabilities, and you want to complete your life without regrets that you didn't accomplish enough.

There was a statistic a while back that showed that people who retired from their careers and didn't have a focused goal, didn't live as long after retirement as those who had definite goals. Life is more interesting when you have a goal to work on.

Another reason to have a big goal is that when you keep focused on the "big picture," it's easier to handle the obstacles along the way. They don't appear so large in relation to your BIG picture/goal.

In Summary: I hope you can apply some of these coaching tips to help you live your dream life---even while you're creating it. It's more fun that way, and it may actually get you there sooner. I also hope the tips have given you a taste of what it's like to be coached.

There will be times in your life when things don't go as planned, when you may feel discouraged, disheartened, or even depressed. Your confidence level may hit new lows and your energy may be zapped. That's when it's great to have a coach who can remind you of your strengths, your accomplishments, and your vision. A coach is there to support you, like a personal cheerleader.

Sometimes it's feedback you need. You think you have a great idea but aren't sure whether to put the time and effort into implementing it. Or you don't know how to implement it. That's when it's good to have someone to bounce ideas off of. A coach can help you determine if your idea is congruent with your overall plan for success and support you if it is.

I hope this gives you some information and motivation to hire a coach for yourself. You can find a listing of coaches to choose from in our Life Coach Directory at www.iaplifecoaches.org/ life-coach-directory.

About the Author

Jeannette Koczela spent several decades as an Impressionist oil painter and working as a free-lance artist. Then an interest in computers led her to become a graphic and web designer, and to create online products including a flash card set, and a home study course, which included some coaching.

Intrigued by the new field of life coaching, she took a certified spiritual life coach training and began coaching coaches. While interacting with life coaches, she began to see a need for more ways for them to connect with potential clients and to learn more business skills. The idea of founding an association culminated in creating her "International Association of Professional Life Coaches®."

The association offers an online directory, monthly business and marketing training packages and coaching calls, opportunities for publishing and speaking, and other business resources for life coaches.

She is the author of three books about marketing for coaches and publisher of five best-selling business books.

Get a free Life Coach Business Toolkit at
www.iaplifecoaches.org/tools

Personal website: www.jeannettekoczela.com
Association website: www.iaplifecoaches.org
Email: jeannettekoczela@iaplifecoaches.org

The International Association of Professional Life Coaches® (IAPLC)

Visibility ~ Credibility ~ Connection

The IAPLC is an organization for life coaches to list their services and for others to find a life coach. Members must meet certain criteria to be listed. As an international professional association dedicated exclusively to the life coaching industry it has membership standards based on training, coaching experience and client references.

To find a life coach: Our user-friendly online directory has listings of life coaches in over 15 different categories. Anyone seeking a life coach will find all the information they need to aid them in selecting a coach. The directory can be found at www.iaplifecoaches.org/life-coach-directory

At the bottom of that page you will also find our *"Find a Coach Guide"* that you can download.

To become a member: The association combines a premier user-friendly international online directory with group business-building activities for its members so they can grow their coaching businesses and get more clients.

To become a member, visit:
www.iaplifecoaches.org/membership